Three
Priorities
for a
Strong Local
Church

Stephen, my
brother —

on your sabbatical
with joy. Have a
blast

By Ray Ortlund

Reach for Life
Lord, Make My Life a Miracle
Lord, Make My Life Count
Intersections
Circle of Strength
Three Priorities for a Strong Local Church

By Ray and Anne Ortlund

The Best Half of Life
Staying Power

By Anne Ortlund

Disciplines of the Beautiful Woman
Discipling One Another
Disciplines of the Heart
Joanna: A Story of Renewal
Up with Worship
Children Are Wet Cement
Building a Great Marriage

*What are the secrets for a vital,
growing Christian Community?*

Ray
Ortlund

Three
Priorities
for a
Strong Local
Church

with Built-in Study Guide

WORD PUBLISHING
Dallas · London · Vancouver · Melbourne

THREE PRIORITIES FOR A STRONG LOCAL CHURCH
formerly published as
LET THE CHURCH BE THE CHURCH

Library of Congress Cataloging in Publication data:

Ortlund, Raymond C.
  Let the church be the church.

  1. Church. 2. Christian leadership. 2. Ortlund,
Raymond C. I. Title.
BV600.2.077   1983   230   83-10375
ISBN 0-8499-0340-8
ISBN 0-8499-3101-0

Unless otherwise noted, all Scripture quotations are from the New International Version of the Bible, copyright © 1978 by New York International Bible Society, and are used by permission. Scriptures marked KJV are from the King James Version of the Bible. Scriptures marked TLB are from *The Living Bible, Paraphrased* (Wheaton: Tyndale House Publishers, 1971) and are used by permission.

Printed in the United States of America

3 4 5 6 7 8 9 LBM 7 6 5 4 3 2

*This book is gratefully dedicated
to the first church of which I was pastor,
whose people lovingly launched me
into the ministry of Christ:*

*THE LATTA MEMORIAL PRESBYTERIAN CHURCH
CHRISTIANA, PENNSYLVANIA*

Contents

PROLOGUE

Dealing with the three priorities together, their
biblical basis, how they interrelate, and how they
influence both church and individual lifestyle.
Chapters 1–6   9

SECTION ONE: OUR FIRST PRIORITY—CHRIST

A. The first priority in the public life of a church.
Chapters 7–10   31

B. The first priority in the private life of
a church leader.
Chapters 11–12   42

SECTION TWO: OUR SECOND PRIORITY—
THE BODY OF CHRIST

A. The second priority in the public life of a church.
Chapters 13–18   55

B. The second priority in the private life of
a church leader.
Chapters 19–20   79

SECTION THREE: OUR THIRD PRIORITY—
THE WORLD

A. The third priority in the public life of a church.
Chapters 21–25   91

B. The third priority in the private life of
a church leader.
Chapter 26   108

EPILOGUE

Symbolism: Why the three priorities are important
to define, to mobilize, to motivate. The role of
the Christian leader.
Chapters 27–28   111
Study Guide   123

Three
Priorities
for a
Strong Local
Church

Prologue

1.

Has your church really become part of "the church"—or did it just steal the label?

When the church truly becomes the church it starts fulfilling God's original intentions for it.

Think about it.

Some churches are merely *evangelistic centers.* All that's done during the week and even on Sunday mornings is leading up to the altar call! That's the focus of the entire life of the church—that exciting moment at five minutes to twelve every Sunday—and it's wonderful to see people walk the aisle and acknowledge a decision of some kind. But did God preordain his church primarily for that?

Some churches are first of all *mission centers.* There's the thermometer up in front and the map on the wall, and people talk a lot about fifty-fifty budgets, and they hear a lot of missionary reports from the pulpit. Certainly any local body is to spread the Good News outward in every possible way, but was that God's chief intention for the church?

Some churches are first of all *information centers.* Their main purpose is to pour out biblical material, and the buzz words are *teach* and *teacher.* The people come to fill their notebooks and their heads, and the ones with fat notebooks and full heads are the spiritual winners. (No, I didn't say what you thought I said!)

But is that God's idea of the church's highest function?

Some churches are mainly *program centers.* They are platforms—stages, really—which seek to have one extravaganza after another. They say, "Man, if you thought this Sunday was good, just wait till next week! We're going to have a gospel magician, three singing groups, and a ventriloquist who will blow your mind!" But did God's eternal plan mean for Christianity merely to be equivalent to Christian "show biz"?

Some churches are *fellowship centers,* where the emphasis is on "body life" and relational theology and discipling and small groups and the function of gifts and all that. Relationships are exciting and good, but was this God's first goal for his church when he planned for it before the foundation of the world?

Or some churches are *counseling centers* or *rescue missions* or *training schools.* All these are good, and all may be part of what we seek to do or be. But do these functions achieve God's central focus for the church?

The Lord ordained the church for himself. The church's chief function, as also the individual believer's function, is to glorify God and to enjoy him forever. He himself must be the church's first priority!

"May . . . God . . . give you a spirit of unity among yourselves as you follow Christ Jesus, so that with one heart and mouth you may glorify the God and Father of our Lord Jesus Christ" (Rom. 15:5,6).

"In him we were also chosen . . . in order that we . . . might be for the praise of his glory" (Eph. 1:11,12).

"And he is the head of the body, the church . . . so that in everything he might have the supremacy" (Col. 1:18).

". . . so that the name of our Lord Jesus may be glorified in you . . ." (2 Thess. 1:12).

"Through Jesus, therefore, let us continually offer to God a sacrifice of praise" (Heb. 13:15).

"You are chosen people . . . that you may declare the praises of him who called you out of darkness into his wonderful light" (1 Pet. 2:9).

The church is for Christ! Then let the church be the church—its activities all determinedly focused on him, its adherents all lovingly gathered around him, and its hearty praises ascending as continual incense to him!

With that first priority fixed steadfastly before our eyes will come obedience to what he says. Then we'll see that the church is to reach upward, to reach within, and to reach out:

1. to glorify him,
2. to build each other up in love, and
3. to evangelize the world.

But *the second and third functions will fall into place only when the first is seen to be—and faithfully practiced as—first.*

Examine with me the ground rules for the church universal—and let's get back to the business of being the church!

2.

I can't remember when I didn't feel called into the ministry. I didn't always *like* the idea, but I knew it was inevitable—that God wanted me to be a pastor.

I was born into a Swedish-American congregation in Des Moines, Iowa, and my earliest memories are of being a little kid ramming around the church getting into trouble! The church people—those who weren't actual relatives—were at least psychologically a kind of "extended family."

And they all had a part in raising me. One of my spinster aunts particularly felt it her calling to keep me spanked into shape; one time when I was misbehaving she took me out of church and into the men's room (it was closest) and whaled the daylights out of me.

But I knew I was loved. And another of the memories is of when Peter Englund, a godly old saint there, tousled my hair with his fingers and said, "Raymond, some day God's going to make you a preacher." I knew it was true, and that awesome moment seemed like my ordination to me—with his kind old hand on my blond head, and his words of reality in my ears.

It wasn't all easy. Navy duty during World War II interrupted my college. . . .

But in June of 1950, there I was at last in cap and gown with Anne at my side. At least she was at my side when the parents took pictures. Otherwise we were both chasing Sherry, not much past three, in one direction, or Margie, not much past two, in another, while taking turns carrying Buddy, aged almost one.

And so to our first pastorate, a lovely stone Presbyterian church in the green farmlands of Lancaster County, Pennsylvania. I walked to my study in the church for a couple of hours early mornings, home to breakfast and back again till noon, and afternoons I did visitation and other pastoral duties. The people were kind to put up with my early mistakes, and among so many who were kind to us, a lady named Dorothy Martin slipped a lot of pies in the back door, and babysat so Anne could join me at church meetings. Bless her heart!

In those days I'd never heard of Peter Drucker. You probably know that he's a management expert who's consulted with many churches and Christian organizations, and that his first question to them is always, "What are you trying to accomplish?"

In the thirty-three years since going to that first village church I've thought a lot about this. It seems that churches, as Drucker says, are not so much in a crisis of organization as they are in a crisis of objectives.[1]

How can the church be the church?

The great danger most churches face is not that they don't do anything—they do plenty. It's that they don't do the right things.

And the great danger that most *pastors* face is not that they don't do anything; their legs are run off of them! It's that they don't do the essential things.

Have you heard the story of the pilot who announced over his intercom system, "Ladies and gentlemen, I have good news and bad news. The good news is that we have a tailwind, and we are making excellent time. The bad news is that our compass is broken, and we have no idea where we are going."

That situation is true of many, probably most, churches—because it's true of many, probably most, pastors.

This is not a "put down." I honor those servants of God who want with all their hearts to serve God well. But we are all so prone to getting confused and losing direction.

The issue is not that God's promises to the church are inadequate. Marcus Dods in his *Expositor's Bible* expands on God's statement, "I am the Almighty God," with these beautiful words:

> I am the Almighty God, able to fulfill your highest hopes and accomplish for you the brightest ideal that ever my words set before you. There is no need for paring down the promise until it squares with human probabilities, no need of adopting some interpretation of it which may make it seem easier to fulfill, and no need of striving to fulfill it in any second-rate way.
>
> All possibility lies in this: I am the Almighty God.[2]

I have to tell you that through all the hard work, bright moments, rejections, triumphs and frustrations of four pastorates, God's plans for me have not been *less* than my hopes and dreams, but far *more.*

Dods says it so well: "For our complaint is not that God gives so little but that he offers too much, more than we care to have: That he never lets us be content with anything short of what perfectly fulfills his perfect love and purpose."[3]

He can be trusted! He can be believed in! His promises for his church are absolutely vast! And *the church is equipped with every power to fulfill every objective God has for it.* Will you believe that? Let your expectation soar to every height, plumb every depth, and accomplish every goal carved out in the mind of God.

There was a time when the famous Dr. Charles Spurgeon was talking to a young preacher, "feeling him out," and he said, "You really don't expect much to happen in your pastorate, do you?"

The fellow said, "Well,—no . . ."

And Dr. Spurgeon almost exploded, "Then you won't *see* much happen, either!"

Ask God to give you the precious gift of high expectations for your church.

3.

What ought to be the goals of a local church? What should the staff and leaders decide on as their church's biblical objectives? How do they get their people committed to the right things? How do they get their local fellowship prioritized?

Unless we ask this question we'll aim at nothing—and hit it every time! Many a pastor thinks he's served a church five years or ten years, when actually he's served only one year and repeated his one-year pastorate five times over or ten times over. He has little sense of direction, of going anywhere, and he doesn't lead his people strongly.

It is important that churches, pastors, staffs, church leaders develop a philosophy of ministry, a direction, a definition of who they are and where they're going together. "What is needed today are congregations that understand their unique purpose as a church and concentrate on fulfilling that function."[4]

We've got to "eliminate and concentrate"! We've got to decide what's important and strengthen that, to pare away all the "stuff" that clutters and confuses, that takes our time and saps our strength. This is true for churches, and it's true for pastors and church leaders.

A decade ago I asked the leaders of the church I was pastoring at the time, "What are the biblical priorities? What are the basics for a local Christian church that are absolutely rock-bottom—whether it exists in the year two hundred A.D. or two thousand A.D., whether it is a church of fifty people or ten thousand?"

For many months we worked on a philosophy of ministry, and I believe that God in his Word revealed to us this pattern, this shape, for the goals of any church, anywhere, anytime:

1. We are to be committed first to Jesus Christ,
2. We are to be committed to one another in Christ, and
3. We are to be committed to the world Christ died to save.

Anne tells me that the first morning I challenged our congregation to these three commitments[5] she was sitting in her pew thinking, "Yes, and M–O–T–H–E–R spells 'mother,' and 'a boy's best friend is his dog,' and what else is new?" The three commitments seemed obvious and trite to the point of being boring.

But the truth is, the practical application of these three priorities is revolutionary, and that morning God performed a stroke of genius: he had me insist from the first that those three priorities be measurably applied. *In that lies the whole secret.*

It was early October, and I said, "If you dear friends will commit yourselves to these three priorities, will you 'put feet' on your commitment?

"If you will recommit yourself to God, will you seek to have a quiet time with him every day from now until Easter?

"If you will recommit yourself to the body of Christ, will you get together in a weekly small group that will meet from now until Easter?

"If you will recommit yourself to this needy world, will you seek to love one person to Christ and into membership in this church by next Easter?

"If you'll agree to all three, please sign a registration card to tell me so, and very soon on a Sunday afternoon we'll meet for an accountability time for you to report who your small group is. This will give you a support base of prayer to help you live out the first and third priorities as well."

Six hundred people signed, and they became the core of a movement that penetrated and revolutionized the whole church in those days.

These three priorities must be kept in order. We must not let our ministry to the world, our evangelism and good works become of first importance. We must not let our fellowship and intrachurch functioning be first. To the extent that Priority Three becomes Priority One—or Priority Two becomes first—we will be out of kilter, out of God's plan, and we'll become fussing, uptight, confused and tired. We'll be "just another church," half-heartedly serving God in such a way as not to offend the devil! We'll collectively waste millions of dollars soaked unnecessarily into real estate, and waste untold numbers of man-hours, of the members' time and energy, as they fiddle their way through unnecessary motions.

Anne and I had Sunday brunch a while back with the former executive officer of the ruling board of a local church. Of the church laymen he was the "main man." He told about hassling his way through hundreds of hours of debates and nitpicking, thinking that was the sacrifice people were supposed to make to serve the Lord.

Then one night late into the hours of a board meeting, after grinding through the usual tensions—to his own complete surprise, he resigned! He said a written letter of confirmation would follow, and he simply got up and walked out.

He never looked back. He never attended that church again. And in the months that followed, he found Jesus Christ as his personal Savior and has since been seeking to learn in another local body what a church is really supposed to do to be the church. That's an exciting pilgrimage!

4.

First comes Christ.

Then comes one another in Christ.

Then comes the world for whom Christ died—our work in it, our service for it, our witness to it.

These three commitments are not hatched out of human brains. Any man-made list of priorities would be sure to stress whatever happened to be weak in a particular culture at that particular period of time. No, these three priorities shine repeatedly from the pages of Scripture. They are deeply, fundamentally planted in the heart of God.

We even find that they're the three subjects of concern when God the Son prayed to God the Father, just before the cross. In John 17,

1. Jesus prayed in verses 1 to 5 for his Father's glory, and that the Son would also be glorified.

2. In verses 6 through 20 he prayed for "the men you gave me," the disciples, for their protection and sanctification—and for us believers to follow.

3. Finally, in verses 21 to the end, he prayed for the world to believe and know the truth.

And we find that Jesus commanded these same three priorities of us. In John 15,

1. He says in verses 1 through 11 that we are to abide in him, and in his love.

2. The middle section, verses 12 through 17, commands us to love each other; it even begins and ends with those words.

3. Last, in verses 18 to the end, he describes our relationship to a hostile world and says we are to witness to it when the Holy Spirit is given to us.

Christ.

One another in Christ.

The world for whom Christ died.

These loves, these commitments, are right for every individual Christian. And they must be modeled by church pastors and leaders. When I have a lot of items to do for the day and wonder what to tackle next, I must prioritize them. Have I had my quiet time that day? No? Then everything else must wait. Are there things to do that will build up the body of Christ? Let them come next. Have I crowded out witnessing to my unsaved neighbor lately? Let's not put it off any longer; desk work can wait.

These loves, these commitments (to Christ, to believers, and to the world), are right for every married couple, every family. Their first order of business needs to be allegiance to Christ— the worship of him, family devotions, bringing up the children to love the Lord—and so on.

Then the family together must love the church and serve it! Our own family is a happy example of this, though we've made lots of mistakes and I don't want to appear simplistic and slick. The first church I served had no nursery facilities, and Sherry, Margie, and Buddy were three, two, and one. They sat on lots of hard pews, played on the sidelines of many committee meetings, and partook of endless potlucks! How did all that affect them? They grew up feeling close to us and fiercely loyal to the local church which we all served together. They are all involved in ministry today. (Nels, born much later, is still in college at this point.)

And every household grouping needs a love for the world. Maps, pennies and prayers for missions, having missionaries in the home, loving concern for the neighbors down the street who don't know Jesus—all these expand the spirits and horizons of families together.

These three loves, these commitments, are right for every small group. Seeing God as its first priority will cause a group not to be merely horizontal but also vertical, with a Christ-focus. Then the members will seek to meet each other's needs, and rather than being exclusive they'll look for outreach as a group project.

One of the exciting small groups Anne and I have belonged to met three Thursday nights a month. On the remaining Thursday night we were the core group of an evangelistic Bible study for non-Christians, and together we saw many friends come to Christ.

These loves, these commitments, are right for every local church. The highest need and responsibility of local churches is to exalt and obey the Lord. Then they need to nourish each other, and to let their Priority Two commitment spread to the body of Christ worldwide, in cooperation and attitudes of respect. Then they must reach to the lost, in projects that range from home-base "guest events" to planting churches on the opposite side of the globe.

These loves, these commitments, are right for every missions organization. I know of two which are deliberately built on the three priorities, ministering with great effectiveness first to the Lord, then to each other, and then to the lost. And many missionary groups and some Christian colleges have experienced revival when they made fresh commitments to these three priorities.

These loves, these commitments, are the right orientation for any Christian grouping of from two to millions. Small churches grow as new people are attracted to a positive, wholesome love for God, for each other, and for the world. Large churches stay warm and personal as they worship and care for the saved and care for the lost.

Some people have asked, "Where does the family fit into these priorities?"—as though the family must compete for time and attention.[6] That's like asking, "Where do *I* fit into these priorities?" No, every individual believer must be committed to Christ, to his body, and to the world. And every family, every church, every grouping in his name must be committed to loving all three.

These three loves seem obvious and trite, don't they? In theory they are unthreatening, even innocuous. But in practice they challenge everything we have. And, at least in my limited observation, if followed they can pave the way to continuous renewal.

5.

Several years after I had begun to preach these three priorities, the chairman of our church trustees said to his board, "Gentlemen, if we say we believe in the three priorities, why do we start our meetings with a brief word of Scripture and prayer and then get to business? We ought to give at least half our time to worship, to Priority One, and then to caring for each other, reporting on our joys and sorrows and supporting one another in prayer. Then let's balance our time together by doing the business at hand."

It seemed a dangerous commitment of time, but the men agreed to give it a try. To their amazement, not only did they learn to love God and each other more, but they finished their business in the same time they always had! Oiled by the Holy Spirit, the machinery of trustee work clicked along without undue stress, indecision or disagreements. And it was interesting that when a trustee would feel the first half was less important and walk in late, his uptightness would be obvious to all, and he'd be an irritant to the group!

News of the trustees' experiment trickled through the church, and before long this became the policy, more or less, of all the church boards and committees—with the hand of God upon the church in deep blessing.

Not long after the trustees began restructuring their meetings, Anne and I flew with a team of two laymen to minister to the missionaries of the Colombia-Panama Branch of Wycliffe Bible Translators at their Colombian jungle base.

We were to be there during the entire ten-day annual gathering of the Branch—some hundred or so missionaries. The first Friday through Sunday we would conduct an intensive "spiritual life" weekend. Then Monday through the next Sunday the Branch would spend the daytime hours electing its officers, hearing tribal reports, and making financial and policy decisions. Evenings, the team would carry on.

That first weekend, as we spelled out the three priorities, we mentioned how the trustees back home were apportioning their meeting times.

On Sunday night the missionaries said, "Why shouldn't we do that, too? Let's have the team keep on leading us in worship and caring for each other and so on for five full days, and ask God to help us do all our annual business in the other five days!"

It seemed a crazy leap of faith, but everyone agreed. The days went by like a bit of heaven on earth. Then Wednesday morning they plunged happily into their business—and by the end of Friday they were through! Every decision had been made on its first vote, "slick as grease."

The ramifications of that annual meeting continued for months, some say years. A missionary couple who had been so discouraged they were ready to quit stayed on with great success. A church back home repented of not having backed in prayer one floundering missionary, and saw him experience a great turnaround. And one tribe well known for its resistance to the gospel became almost totally Christian.

I'm sure God uses many forces to make these things happen. But this I know to be true: in the atmosphere of sincerely committing our lives together to Christ, to each other, and to our work, roadblocks come down and ministry goes on in power.

6.

These three priorities are not to be "done" chronologically, one at a time. ("I can't lead anyone to Christ yet; I have to learn to worship first.") No, all three are to be the most fundamental part of our lives all the time.

And they will form their own distinctive lifestyle for any Christian, for any church. It will not be the same lifestyle in Africa as in Tennessee, and it will not be the same lifestyle in 1810 A.D. as in 1994—and yet both believers or group of believers if they could see each other, would understand and appreciate each other. The three commitments allow for powerful creativity and enormous variety as the Spirit leads, and yet the lifestyle they produce will be unique and recognizably distinctive. Christians obedient to these three commitments will see similar, authentically biblical and godly characteristics emerge.

Equally important, steadfast commitment to these three priorities will keep Christians or churches from getting into endless numbers of areas where they don't belong. Jesus' statement, "Let the dead bury the dead," seems limiting, confining, and maybe unnecessarily severe. But the devil knows how distrac-

25

tions will get us off balance, upset, negative, and hostile, and he'll lure us into substitute commitments every time if he can do it.

Loving God, loving each other, loving the world—these three priorities can keep us innovative and challenged and occupied in happy, healthy, positive, aggressive ways.

They can bring us past the reactionisms into which young Christians, young pastors, young churches, and young movements are likely to fall. I was talking to a pastor recently who described to me his pilgrimage out of a narrow, suspicious background, through squabbles within his denomination over modes of baptism or where money was to be given, through painful fights over doctrinal issues, organizational issues . . . He'd been through years of "Christian civil wars." We agreed together that growth demands these things must be eventually settled in our minds, but that we can't begin really to minister as church leaders or as churches until we've gotten past being reactionary.

Focusing on the three priorities fastens blinders on us to keep us from side issues, from the non-eternal, from the unworthy. The writer to the Hebrews was not denying that opinions have to be settled concerning basic issues, and yet he said, "Let us leave the elementary teachings about Christ and go on to maturity, not laying again the foundation of repentance from acts that lead to death, and of faith in God, instruction about baptisms, the laying on of hands, the resurrection of the dead, and eternal judgment" (6:1,2).

In other words, "settle those things and get on to the large, positive, grand concerns for which God ordained us!" In our thinking, in our functioning, let the church be the church!

See how broad are the three priorities! The concept of loving God, loving those in the faith, and loving those outside the faith span the whole Bible—Old Testament as well as New.

The Old Testament is filled with Priority One:

"I am the Lord your God. . . . You shall have no other gods before me" (Exod. 20:2,3).

"Hear, O Israel: The Lord our God, the Lord is one. Love

the Lord your God with all your heart and with all your soul and with all your strength" (Deut. 6:4,5).

"I will praise you, O Lord, with all my heart" (Ps. 9:1).

The Old Testament is filled with Priority Two:

"Do not defraud your neighbor or rob him. . . . Do not go about spreading slander among your people. . . . Do not hate your brother in your heart. . . . but love your neighbor as yourself" (Lev. 19:13,16–18).

"Be openhanded toward your brothers . . ." (Deut. 15:11).

"You may charge a foreigner interest, but not a brother Israelite . . ." (Deut. 23:20).

"You should not look down on your brother in the day of his misfortune . . ." (Obad. 12).

"Administer true justice; show mercy and compassion to one another. . . . In your hearts do not think evil of each other" (Zech. 7:8–10).

The Old Testament is filled with Priority Three:

"All peoples of the earth will be blessed through you" (God to Abram, Gen. 12:3).

"May your ways be known on earth, your salvation among all nations" (Ps. 67:2).

"I will make [Israel] a light for the Gentiles, that you may bring my salvation to the ends of the earth" (Isa. 49:6).

And the New Testament is filled with Priority One:

"For from him and through him and to him are all things. To him be the glory forever! Amen" (Rom. 11:36).

"Praise be to the God and Father of our Lord Jesus Christ" (Eph. 1:3).

". . . to the praise of his glory" (Eph. 1:14).

"Fix your thoughts on Jesus" (Heb. 3:1).

"Let us fix our eyes on Jesus" (Heb. 12:2).

"May he work in us what is pleasing to him" (Heb. 13:20).

. . . And into a crescendo of focused worship through the book of Revelation even to the final page, when John, in the typical human temptation to wander off into doublemindedness, falls down to worship at the feet of the angel who had shown him the revelation, and the angel says, "Do not do it!

I am a fellow servant with you. . . . Worship God!" (Rev. 22:8,9).

The New Testament is filled with Priority Two:

"A new commandment I give you: Love one another" (John 13:34).

"Accept one another, then, just as Christ accepted you" (Rom. 15:7).

"Love is patient, love is kind. It does not envy, it does not boast, it is not proud." (1 Cor. 13:4).

"Carry each other's burdens . . ." (Gal. 6:2).

"From him the whole body, joined and held together by every supporting ligament, grows and builds itself up in love, as each part does its work" (Eph. 4:16).

"Make my joy complete by being like-minded, having the same love, being one in spirit and purpose. Do nothing out of selfish ambition or vain conceit, but in humility consider others better than yourselves" (Phil. 2:2,3).

"Bear with each other, and forgive . . ." (Col. 3:13).

And on and on!

Nor does the New Testament slight the third priority.

"God did not send his Son into the world to condemn the world, but to save the world through him" (John 3:17).

"You will be my witnesses . . ." (Acts 1:8).

"Always be prepared to give an answer to everyone who asks you to give the reason for the hope that you have" (1 Pet. 3:15).

"Be wise in the way you act toward outsiders; make the most of every opportunity" (Col. 4:5).

"I urge, then . . . that requests, prayers . . . be made for everyone—for kings and all those in authority. . . . This is good, and pleases God our Savior, who wants all men to be saved and to come to a knowledge of the truth" (1 Tim. 2:1-4).

Let our chief concerns be in harmony with God's concerns! Let our philosophy of ministry be synchronized with his own heart! Let our burdens reflect his burdens; let the church be the church!

Section One
OUR FIRST PRIORITY—

CHRIST

Part A:
The first priority in the public life of a church

7.

Are you ready for a new, old, revolutionary, deeply-rooted, biblical, mind-boggling idea for your church?

In your corporate life put Jesus Christ first.

That's it.

His presence, his lordship must be taken with total seriousness.

The Scriptures cry out that at the top, at the center, in the front, and underneath everything is Christ. He is supreme in the universe—whether all of nature yet recognizes it or not. He is supreme in the church—whether local Christians and congregations live it out or not.

But to the extent that he is not yet Lord of all creation, that creation "groans as in the pains of childbirth" (Rom. 8:22). And to the extent that Christ is not yet total Lord of the church, we will be hassled, confused, quarrelsome, and exhausted.

The priority of the Lord Jesus Christ is not a "first" truth that you leave when you go on to deeper teaching. You cannot as a Christian or as a body of believers ever get beyond this.

You must live every aspect of your life in the light of it. You must deal with it all your life, or it will deal with you.

Every Christian church or denomination states in some way in its creed that Christ is Lord and Head over all that the people are and do. But many have gotten into theological and practical confusion because his lordship was not conscientiously recognized and practiced. Clear direction comes from total acknowledgment of him "in all our ways" (see Prov. 3:5,6).

This takes constant attention and a whole lifetime to live out and experience. Is your church willing to admit the possibility that in some areas of its life he is indeed not yet preeminent?

There came a time after I'd been pastor of Lake Avenue Congregational Church for about twelve years that we seemed to be settling, waning. I think the morale of the congregation as a whole was good; but to me, as the one who watched over them to "give an account," (Heb. 13:17), we seemed too horizontal in our thinking and doing. Some of us drew aside to pray and ask the question I just posed: were we willing to admit the possibility that in some areas of our church life Christ was indeed not yet preeminent? What were the areas?

We thought we'd better ask *him*—together as a congregation. So we had a week of "waiting on God."[7] There were no programs, no plans made. We simply cancelled everything (a big job in a big church!), ground all the machinery to a halt, and gathered each evening for a week to sit before the Lord and see what he would say to us.

Maybe Quakers know a lot about this, but I tell you, for us activist Congregationalists, this was a new thing.

We looked up into his face. We waited on him. Sometimes we were moved to sing, or pray, or confess, or testify. Sometimes we just sat. But that week we became quiet enough to see a lot of things more clearly—especially the Lord. Confessions and adjustments were made. We got cleaned out and restarted—individually, within families, and in our church life.

It was the beginning of a time of prolonged renewal within the church. For several years all the charts and graphs went up—in giving, in attendance, in membership, in missions efforts—following that week of waiting on our God.

After Christ's ascension, the believers did not preach. During the ten days they were together not one person was healed, not one lesson was taught, not one sermon was preached. They had something else to do: to wait on God, to sit quietly until they had his empowering, his direction. The book of Acts has twenty-eight chapters, but only twenty-seven are "acts" or "action" chapters. First there is one chapter of dead stop! And without that important time of waiting for the Spirit's fullness there would have been no Pentecost, no ministry, no Book of Acts, no early church.

There are seasons when the people of God must seek deliberately to put him first, to give him time and attention, to seek his mind and his enabling before they proceed with other activities.

Paul W. Witte, a Roman Catholic, stirred my soul when he wrote,

> I have learned that there is only one truth that can motivate man simply through life: Christ. Before we can consider ourselves Christians we must have believed in Christ and accepted all the consequences of a radically altered life. Without this first basic commitment, growth in Christ through any church structure is impossible.[8]

The most exciting pilgrimage a people can embark on is to seek to keep adjusting and readjusting to Christ and to his firstness.

If a church is centered on anything, anyone, any doctrine, any project—anything but Christ—it is off balance, off center, which means it's "eccentric."[9]

Beware of your church's or your denomination's "distinctives"—your unique qualities—your original reactions which caused your birth! Be scared to death of them! Evangelical churches and groups can become eccentric by being tied to the old or tied to the new—with a subtle haughtiness that tells them they're not "run-of-the-mill."

Traditions of the past, tenaciously clung to, can bind them with chains and drag them downward and away from the fresh firstness of Christ.

Or "kicks" of the present! Churches or leaders can have delusions of being present-day Martin Luthers ("Here I stand; God helping me, I can do no other")—when instead of standing on Luther's broad, grand faith, they're teetering on some silly new little emphasis which in twenty years will have proved not to work and been discarded.

(A church staffer once told me, "Ray, get ready for _____ [a new emphasis]. By next year this thing's gonna be big!" That made me already prejudiced against it. I'd already had all that kind of thing I needed!)

8.

Probably the greatest danger is for a church simply to be centered on itself. Then, whether in its community or around the world, it subtly starts pushing *itself,* not Christ. "The greatest obstacle to evangelization," wrote someone, "is the church which is preoccupied with its own existence."

James Denny wrote, "No man can bear witness to Christ and to himself at the same time. No man can give the impression that he himself is clever and that Christ is mighty to save." I'd like to substitute "the church" in that quotation and amplify it in its own paragraph for you to look at long and hard:

No church can bear witness to Christ and to itself at the same time. No church can give the impression that the church itself is clever [is unique, is the best in the area, has the most baptisms, the best pastor, the most exciting youth or singles ministry, gives the most to missions, is the happiest, most biblical, friendliest, most aggressive, et cetera] and [simultaneously] that Christ is mighty to save.

Any church which does not understand this, no matter how strategically placed, rich, or sharp, is doomed to ultimate confusion.

I see more and more of the Madison Avenue approach in churches' "selling themselves" in their advertising. They're not "holding forth the Word of life" to "a crooked and depraved generation" (see Phil. 2:15,16); they're pushing themselves and their "ministries" (their wares) to attract the attention and the money of the neighborhood or the masses away from other equally pushy churches!

I'm not saying that advertising is wrong, that aggressive evangelism is wrong; they're important to any thriving church. But selling Christ through the vehicle of a local church is a very different thing from playing games of one-upmanship with fellow churches. The Holy Spirit will direct a flock to think up all kinds of exciting, creative ways to promote Jesus without resorting to Madison-Avenue hype and competition.

Beyond and above the flurry and din thunders the Lord God, "I am the Lord; that is my name! I will not give my glory to another or my praise to idols" (Isa. 42:8).

The church exists primarily to *minister to the Lord*—to gather around him, to serve and obey and love and enjoy together the altogether Righteous One, who is worthy of our focus and attention and worship and obedience forever and ever.

Our church life must deliberately revolve around him! Each leader's personal life must deliberately revolve around him! Each family must make him Priority One in the home! Every individual Christian must be taught to do the same—voluntarily, happily, unselfconsciously. This "way" is impossible in the flesh, but it can be achieved gloriously by those who walk in the Spirit.

9.

How does this firstness of God in Christ take its most obvious shape in the life of the body? Certainly in the order and the tone of its corporate worship, as the pastor can and must lead his people in their pursuit of the Lord. The worship service is the "front side" of the church, the side exposed to public view; and the pastor must begin centering on God in the place where the tone is set for the rest of the life of the church.

Isaiah chapter 6 gives a fine order of worship. See the process here of the confrontation between God and man.[10]

First Isaiah saw the Lord in his glory and viewed heavenly beings centering their praise and adoration on him. Let the gathered people of God center their attention first on God himself! The hymns and prayers at the opening part of the service should help God's people adore him (Isa. 6:1–4). Too many times very little thought and prayer are given in preparing the worship service, so that the hymns are inappropriate and the prayers offered without being thought through in advance. Being totally extemporaneous is neither helpful nor spiritual! If a preacher takes care to prepare his message, why

38

shouldn't he or others take equal care with the rest of the service of worship?

When Isaiah saw the Lord he was immediately aware of his own sin and that of his people (Isa. 6:5). Confession of sin must be part of the worship service! Progress is often stopped right here. The worshiping family will never get the full impact of God's blessing without a sense of fresh forgiveness for their sins.

Into every worship service comes a man with great tensions, a girl hurt in her love life, a child worried by arguing parents, a young person newly caught in sin. To their "woe to me" (Isa. 6:5), God wants to respond with cleansing, healing, fresh starts—the assuring words, "your guilt is taken away and your sin atoned for" (Isa. 6:6,7). Each person in a congregation needs to experience this at least weekly!

"Then I heard the voice of the Lord . . ." (Isa. 6:8). The presentation of the message of God in the sermon will be particularly effective if it is preceded by meaningful worship; it will be lifted and enabled by its very context in the service. And every service should lead the worshipers to respond as Isaiah, "Here am I, send me" (Isa. 6:8).

So the sequence of Isaiah 6 is praise and adoration, prayer and confession, presentation of the message, and response. The pastor and church leaders, those who bear "the burden of the Lord," must pray that every Sunday morning the people will meet God! A thin, obviously ill woman once left this message after a certain service: "Tell your people that a stranger stumbled into your church today and found God again."

A people who are taught to love worship in the gathered body on Sundays will allow the habit of worship to trickle down into the rest of church life. In time they will be starting their small groups with worship together—and their choir practices, their Bible studies, even perhaps their social times . . . Worshiping believers are happy believers, at peace with God and with each other.

For years I have kept near me these words of A. E. Whitham to remind me of the desperate need of people, the glorious power and beauty of the Lord Jesus, and the wonder of the privilege of putting the two together:

> If you knew that there was one greater than yourself, who knows you better than you can know yourself, and loves you better than you can love yourself, who can make you all you ought to be, steadier than your squally nature, able to save you from squandering your glorious life, who searches you beyond the standards of earth . . . one who gathered into himself all great and good things and causes, blending in his beauty all the enduring color of life, who could turn your dreams into visions, and make real the things you hoped were true; and if that one had ever done one unmistakable thing to prove, even at the price of blood—his own blood—that you could come to him, and having failed, come again,
>
> Would you not fall at his feet with the treasure of your years, your powers, service, and love? And is there not one such, and does he not call you . . .?[11]

10.

The God-centered church must be willing to put all its activities on trial before the judgment seat of the Lord. Is it all for him?

Some time ago our church staff and I surveyed again all the activities of our church, and recommended to the proper boards and committees that certain ones be eliminated. We just didn't feel they were consistent with our church's philosophy of ministry, which stated that Christ was first and that all must enhance his preeminence. So several programs were cut off.

Other recommendations were that the planning of the worship services be given quality time by several of our most gifted leaders, and that all those in any kind of active service in the church set the example in Priority One by careful attendance in the worship services. How, we asked, could leaders enjoy and promote the Christ-centered life, as our philosophy of ministry stated, if they didn't take part in regular worship with the people of God?

Christ is first priority! Those who live out their personal and corporate life with that truth will experience holy revolution. He must be central, pervading everything. If that seems trite, or too abstract and mystical—the fact remains that when this truth is taken seriously, its ramifications in any local church will become exciting and creative and fresh.

He must be all in your experience, even though he is all in your theology. Toward him all must move, in quiet reverence. There is only one way. It is the self-chosen surrender of all you do, and the way you do it, to Jesus Christ—so that you all sit together in the shadows of his glory.

Who knows, then, how committees or choirs will break into worship? Who knows what church boards will sense disagreement on some issue and quit everything to seek the Lord's mind? Who knows who will be in quiet fasting and prayer behind the scenes, that God may be more magnified in the church's public life? What future projects and goals will the Spirit project, as old men dream dreams and young men see visions? (see Joel 2:28).

Pastors and church leaders will have to walk softly and not "control" everything, as the Holy Spirit inspires godly creativity to bubble up. Their hand of leadership will be needed mostly, by example and by teaching, to steer their flock's energies into three channels—loving God, loving each other, and loving the world. And then to warn, to chide, to correct when lesser issues become too important. And most of all, to rejoice as undershepherds when Christ himself is in fact given charge to lead his church!

Lancelot Andrewes prayed a prayer for individuals that we can translate for the nitty-gritty, day-by-day workings of any local church. It will transform how the pastors spend their time, the attitudes of secretaries and custodians, the program of the music department!

> Be Lord,
> within us to strengthen us,
> without us to guard us,
> over us to shelter us,
> beneath us to establish us,
> before us to guide us,
> after us to forward us,
> around us to secure us.[12]

Part B:

The first priority in the private life of a church leader

11.

When a church leader (pastor or otherwise) involves himself deeply enough, and for a long enough time, in the life of the congregation, his personality, his thinking, his emphasis will all shape the life of the flock.

There is absolutely no way a church or Christian organization or work of any kind can become authentically Christ-centered and whole and balanced unless its leadership is Christ-centered and whole and balanced! Followers never become what their leader is not.

On the other hand, a busy, rushing pastor will produce a busy, rushing church.

A work-oriented mission head will produce a work-oriented mission.

Rigid, hard, legalistic church officers produce rigid, hard, legalistic church members.

Soft, emotional, untheological leadership produces a soft, emotional, untheological congregation.

Oh, that Christ may indeed hold the leadership of your church in his hand, as he did the "angels," "messengers," leaders of the seven churches in the book of Revelation!

It is essential that Jesus Christ be dynamically first in the personal life of a spiritual leader. With Christ at the center there is movement, rearrangement, direction, empowering. Christ is a class all by himself, and you worship Christ. You bow in reverence to him. Behind the scenes of your life, Christ must be Lord! You must stake your all on him.

Your wife or your husband can't be first. She or he can only be a companion on the way, and then at the last you let go your hands and move into eternity one-on-one with God.

Your children can't be first. Eventually, to escape that kind of pressure, they would bolt from home.

Scholarship can't be first. To let the symbols of learning, the degrees, the publications, the knowledge and studying become too important is fleshly; it's idolatrous; to God it's vulgar.

Your personal ministry can't be first. You yourself cannot be the glasses through which people are to look to see Christ. If so, when you're not there, they can't find him!

Your church can't be first. If you're occupied primarily with its life and its functions, you'll be too exhilarated over its successes and too discouraged over its failures. You'll think horizontally; you'll talk politically; you won't be drawing on the deep resources of the Spirit, and sooner or later you'll experience burnout.

And you yourself can't be first. You were made to put Jesus first, and you'll only function well in that way! "Seek ye [be seeking continually, in ever-fresh ways] first the kingdom of God, and his righteousness; and all these things shall be added unto you" (Matt. 6:33, KJV).

Fromke said it so well:

Believers may not often realize it, but even as believers we are either centered on man, or centered on God. There is no alternative. Either God is the center of our universe and we have become rightly adjusted to him, or we have made ourselves the center and are attempting to make all else orbit around us and for us.[13]

To get balance in your own life you must be very sure that Christ is supreme. Any overemphasis, any overreaction will make you temporarily off balance, and you must go back and back to the person of Christ—back and back to thinking of him, devotion to him, studying him, worshiping him—and ministering him to others.

The Christian leader's primary task must be to join David in his words of Psalms 103:1: "Praise the Lord, O my soul; all my inmost being, praise his holy name." At every phase of your maturity and growth this will take shape differently, but from this moment on, Christian leader, surrender your heart to seek to do this. Otherwise your leadership of others will not be truly sincere; it will not be "from the inside out."[14]

> Absolute, personal loyalty to God must take precedence over anything and everything else. . . . All one's ultimate loyalties must converge at a single point. . . . Jesus demanded as an exclusive priority that a person center his life, loyalty, and valuations solely upon God. . . . Every other concern [must] flow out of, fall in behind, and witness to, this one.[15]

Henry Drummond used to warn his theological students regularly, "Don't touch Christianity unless you are willing to seek the Kingdom of Heaven first. I promise you a miserable existence if you seek it second."[16]

Surely this must be the greatest cause of church leadership burnout and dropout! The context of Matthew 6:33 indicates that preoccupation with anything other than God leads to worry. "If God gave man the magnificent gift of life, will he not also do a far simpler thing—sustain that life with every provision?" A church leader who worries and frets has run up a red flag over his head which proclaims, "I have not sought first the kingdom of God. I do not know firsthand his abundant resources, his artesian wells of provision, security, and satisfaction."

So the Christian leader's first and main business is to have a mind set to seek after God. Seeking after things, after the expansion of power and reputation, even after the accumulation of souls as an end rather than a means—Jesus says, "the pagans run after all these things!" (Matt. 6:32). Then the Christian leader gets frantic, he gets crass, he succumbs to the "hard sell." He gets pagan-like.

Martin Lloyd-Jones in his *Studies on the Sermon on the Mount* says, " 'Seek ye first!' That means generally, principally, above everything else; give that priority."[17]

Read again this entry in the diary of David Brainerd, early missionary to the American Indians:

> I found in myself a spirit of love, and warmth, and power, to address the poor Indians. God helped me to plead with them to "turn from all the vanities of the heathen to the living God." I am persuaded the Lord touched their consciences for I never saw such attention raised in them before. And when I came away from them, I spent the whole time, while I was riding to my lodgings three miles distant, in prayer and praise to God.
>
> After I rode more than two miles, it came into my mind to dedicate myself to God again; which I did with great solemnity and unspeakable satisfaction. Especially gave up myself to him renewedly in the work of the ministry. And this I did by divine grace, I hope, without any exception or reserve; not the least shrinking back from any difficulties that might attend this great and blessed work. I seemed to be most free, cheerful and full in this dedication of myself. My whole soul cried: "Lord, to thee I dedicate myself! Oh, accept of me and let me be thine forever. Lord, I desire nothing else; I desire nothing more. Oh, come, come, Lord, accept a poor worm. 'Whom have I in heaven but Thee? and there is none upon earth, that I desire besides Thee.' "[18]

Frederic W. H. Myers' magnificent biography of the apostle Paul in poetry says it this way:

> Christ's! I am Christ's! And let that Name suffice you;
> Aye, for me too He greatly hath sufficed.
> Lo, with no winning words I would entice you;
> Paul has no honor and no friend but Christ.[19]

12.

If that's to be the Christian leader's *attitude,* how does his *action* follow? The Bible is full of models; let's take one from the Old Testament.

David models for believers this God-focused life in at least three ways. How wonderful that he wrote so many of the psalms, to let us look so intimately at his heart and life!

First, he says, "I have set the Lord always before me. Because he is at my right hand, I will not be shaken." (Ps. 16:8). Pastors and leaders often get "shook up" over bad news or discouraging circumstances because they have not the determined habit, the godly reflex, of fixing their attention on God! David sought to live with his eyes upward, and he saw life from God's perspective. "Practicing the presence of God" gives emotional health and stability.

For years I've formed the habit of periodically setting my wristwatch alarm to go off at fifteen-minute intervals, as a reminder to "check in with God," to praise him again, to re-"set the Lord always before me." I'm "prone to wander, Lord, I feel it, prone to leave the God I love . . .!"[20] Using my watch alarm as a reminder has helped me as I seek to form the habit of continual inner praise and worship.

How can a leader bring his people where he himself has never been? If it's true (and I believe it is) that "the greatest thing one man can do for another is to bring him to God and leave him there," then a spiritual leader's first job, back behind the scenes, is to live constantly in the presence of God himself.

> The experience is of an invasion from beyond, of an other, who in gentle power breaks in upon our littleness, and in tender expansiveness makes room for himself. Had we thought him an intruder? Nay, his first odor is that of sweetness, his touch an imparting of power.
>
> Suddenly a tender Giant walks by our side,—no, strides within our puny footsteps. We are no longer our little selves.[21]

"My soul finds rest in God alone," sang David in Psalm 62:1—a profound testimony to his authentically spiritual experience—"my salvation comes from him."

The preacher who finds soul rest in that moment-by-moment seeking after God will lead the people past himself to that same God! He will have found for his people the Source of rest and of goodness! Happy the people who come to church not to meet a pastor full of biblical knowledge, but through him to meet God!

> "I walked out to the hill just now," wrote Jim Elliot in his diary. "It is exalting, delicious. To stand embraced by the shadows of a friendly tree with the wind tugging at your coat-tail and the heavens hailing your heart—to gaze and glory and give oneself again to God, what more could a man ask? Oh the fullness, pleasure, sheer excitement of knowing God on earth. I care not if I never raise my voice again for Him, if only I may love Him, please Him. Perhaps in mercy He shall give me a host of children that I may lead them through the vast star fields to explore His delicacies whose finger ends set them to burning. But if not, if

only I may see Him, smell His garments and smile into my Lover's eyes—ah then, not stars nor children shall matter, only Himself."[22]

Second, David loved the sanctuary of God. In the desert of Judah he wrote,

> O God, you are my God,
> earnestly I seek you;
> my soul thirsts for you,
> my body longs for you,
> in a dry and weary land
> where there is no water.
>
> I have seen you in the sanctuary
> and beheld your power and your glory (Ps. 63:1,2).

He comforted his brothers,

> May the Lord answer you when you are in distress. . . .
> May he send you help from the sanctuary
> and grant you support from Zion (Ps. 20:1,2).

He proclaimed, "God has spoken from his sanctuary" (Ps. 60:6) "You are awesome, O God, in your sanctuary" (Ps. 68:35). And he testified, "When I tried to understand [a certain problem], it was oppressive to me till I entered the sanctuary of God" (Ps. 73:16,17).

The summary of his devotion to God's house is perhaps seen in Psalm 27:4:

> One thing I ask of the Lord,
> this is what I seek:
> that I may dwell in the house of the Lord
> all the days of my life,
> to gaze upon the beauty of the Lord
> and to seek him in his temple.

David, hungry for God, knew the depth and power of meeting the Lord in his house in the company of his people.

Third, David formed the habit of secret, regular prayer. 2 Samuel 7:18 says that David "sat before the Lord" and prayed to him. It was a daily thing; in Psalm 5:3 he wrote, "Morning by morning, O Lord, you hear my voice; morning by morning I lay my requests before you and wait in expectation." And in Psalm 55:16,17, when in a time of distress, he said,

> But I call to God,
> and the Lord saves me.
> Evening, morning and noon [the Hebrew day]
> I cry out in distress
> and he hears my voice.

If any Christian leader struggles and fights for a daily time with the Lord, I do. I struggle for it when it doesn't appeal to me, but I struggle for it also when it's the most exciting thing I can think of to do! When my heart is hungry to meet with him, there is still the enormous pressure of things—good, worthy things—to get done.

I know that if, like David, the church leader starts his day with God, then he'll probably more readily live acknowledging his presence all the rest of the day. For correct perspective, time alone with God is essential! And yet the ministry today, for pastor or active layperson, is so demanding that quiet time can easily get crowded out.

Charles Hummel speaks to this:

> The problem is that the important thing rarely has to be done today, or even this week. . . . The urgent tasks are the ones that call for instant action. They seem at the moment to be important and irresistible, so they devour our time and energy.[23]

How wonderful that "reverence for God adds hours to each day" (Prov. 10:27, TLB)! More times than I can number, when at the beginning of an impossible day I have taken time to "sit before the Lord," meetings have been canceled, or I discovered I didn't have an appointment I thought I had. God has done all kinds of creative things to add hours to the day!

And in my heart I know I'm not only settling the deep issues of my own life, but I'm leading the way for other people to settle the deep issues of theirs.

Sometimes Christian leaders need larger hunks of time away with the Lord. Although Jesus had regular times alone with his Father, in times of special need he gave larger portions of time. After a particularly depleting period, he went into the hills for most of the night (Mark 6:44–47). Before making a big decision, he spent a whole night in prayer (Luke 6:12,13).

Inevitably in the life of a Christian leader, as with his people, there will come times of special stress and need. These demand special withdrawal to the Father for answers and for strength.

Anne and I try to have one day a month for what we call "Think Days." We get out of town alone together and do a number of things: worship together, worship separately, critique our marriage, critique our past month, critique our month to come and synchronize our schedules. The busier we are, the more we need these "Think Days" to regroup and get positioned again for the immediate future.

Sometimes a whole people needs to withdraw together. Anne's book, *Up With Worship,* tells of our congregational "weeks of waiting on God,"[24] some of the most crucial times in our spiritual pilgrimage.

If a Christian leader is to help his people become oriented to God, the counsel of David to him or her, then, would include at least three suggestions:

1. Teach believers to live practicing the presence of God.
2. Teach them to worship effectively with the people of God. The local body must experience lofty worship!
3. Teach them how to have personal quiet time.

How does a Christian leader teach these things? I have found it very effective as a pastor to give the congregation the chance not only to *hear* the truth, but then to *do* it. When you preach or speak on a subject, try giving your people "experience time" to act it out on the spot.

Sometimes I have preached on "how to worship in church" at the very beginning of a service, and then we have spent the last two-thirds of the hour going through the service from the prelude on and seeking to put worship into practice.

Or on occasion I have preached, perhaps on a Sunday evening, on how to have a quiet time, and then directed my people in having one right then and there. Christian leaders who are not pastors could use similar strategies in speaking, meeting, or counseling situations.

What it all comes down to is this: If you are a Christian leader—lay or clergy—your life, your preaching or teaching, your methods of leadership must say, "Come, my friends, let's journey together back to what's important. Take your eyes from lesser issues. Whether you've been away from God and his concerns for a long time or for five minutes, it's time for us both to reorient ourselves first of all to him. He is worthy!"

A young fellow was once taken to the top of Lookout Mountain, a peak in the southeast United States famous for its panoramic view of seven states all at once. It was a clear day, and he could see thirty miles in each direction. And it was autumn, with magnificent colorings everywhere. Afterward someone asked him what he saw, and he said, "It was great! I saw the backside of a buzzard."

Church leader, others may give their attention to the inconsequential.

But how about you?

> For the weariest day
>   may Christ be your stay.
> For the darkest night
>   may Christ be your light.
> For the weakest hour
>   may Christ be your power.
> For each moment's fall
>   may Christ be your all.

Section Two
OUR SECOND PRIORITY—

THE BODY
OF CHRIST

Part A:

The second priority in the public life of a church

13.

After World War II, when peaceful communications had been restored between the United States and Japan, one of the first ships to cross the Pacific carried several dozen American missionaries, who had served in Japan before the war and who now were hopefully coming back to take up their work among the people. Their hearts were in their throats, wondering how they would be received!

When at last the ship moored at the Japanese pier, they could see Christians in the crowd on the dock, their faces upturned in eager anticipation. Soon they ran into each other's arms and embraced! Then after they'd caught up on each other's personal news they went to the nearest church and had Communion together.

What is the basis of this kind of human relationship—a relationship which defies all the laws of natural society operating in the strength of the flesh?

God says that his church is of the noblest order, that it has been given love as no other body has love, and that it has the highest possible place in his heart—that it is of ultimate importance to him. And surely we must share God's assessment of his church!

The book of Ephesians shows us four reasons why the church must be our highest priority next to and under our Lord Jesus Christ:

First of all, before all time the church preexisted in the heart of God. Ephesians 1:4: "He chose us in him before the creation of the world."

God anticipated the church. He loved us before we ever were. Ephesians 2:10 calls the church his "workmanship, created in Christ Jesus to do good works, which God prepared in advance for us to do." This is not said of the family, the government, or of any other of God's created institutions.

Second, the church is Jesus Christ's gift to his Father. Ephesians 1:11,18 in the Living Bible says this:

> Moreover, because of what Christ has done we have become gifts to God that he delights in, for as part of God's sovereign plan we were chosen from the beginning to be his, and all things happen just as he decided long ago. . . .

> I want you to realize that God has been made rich because we who are Christ's have been given to him!

Incredible but true! What did God get out of sending his Son to die for our sins? What did he get out of sending his Holy Spirit? He got us! We may look at ourselves and say, "Big deal!" But God says that is a very wonderful thing. Because of the enormous price Jesus paid, before long he will "present you before his glorious presence without fault and with great joy" (Jude 24). The church is Christ's precious gift to his Father, and this is not said of any other institution of God.

Third, the church is Christ's very own body! Jesus is the Head whom the church fulfills and completes, to form the total expression of God! Ephesians 1:23 speaks of the church as "his body, the fullness of him who fills everything in every way."

How awesome! We are in vital union with Jesus Christ! His life flows into us, and the body is the very expression of the Head. Obviously, then, the church is not basically an organization; it's an amazing organism—the completer of the cosmic Christ, and the means to the fullness of his own glory. This is not said of any other institution of God.

Fourth, the church is "number two" after the Lord himself because she is convincing evidence that God is merciful, full of grace, and good. The church is God's evidence before all the universe of his very high character. See Ephesians 2:4–7:

> But because of his great love for us, God, who is rich in mercy, made us alive with Christ even when we were dead in transgressions—it is by grace you have been saved. And God raised us up with Christ and seated us with him in the heavenly realms in Christ Jesus, in order that . . .

[now notice this]

> in the coming ages he might show the incomparable riches of his grace, expressed in his kindness to us in Christ Jesus.

Beings throughout all the universe will soon close their mouths in wonder as they see the church on display as ultimate proof of the goodness of God! This is not said of any other created institution of God.

And so the apostle Paul wraps up his lofty teaching on the church in his writing to the Ephesians by saying,

> To him be glory in the church and in Christ Jesus throughout all generations, for ever and ever! Amen (Eph. 3:21).

Amazing but true: *however weak we may seem at times, the glory of God, the very presence of God, is in his church.* Oh, what a high view of the church we must have and we must teach! In our affections and priorities it must be second only to the Lord himself.

14.

Now of course, the teachings on the church in the book of Ephesians speak of the invisible, mystical body of Christ throughout the ages. But how do you get hold of that except in the local church? Your own church may not be 100 percent genuine, as the worldwide visible church is probably not. (Only God is in the business to know about that for sure.) But the visible church is for now the only church we have to deal with and answer to. The "church at Philippi" or the "church in Cincinnati" is the only laboratory we have in which we can work out our functions as members of Christ's body.

Then we must love it, praise it, protect it, defend it, pray for it, identify with it! Every believer must be a member of a local body of Christ. When a person becomes a Christian, he or she is already a member of Christ's true body; he or she then needs to identify with and fit in with real flesh-and-blood people.

The Christian who never gets together with other believers before God, to pray and share and serve so that he is known as he knows them, is not an obedient Christian. He is not in the will of God. However vocal he may be in his testimony, however straight he may be in his theology, he is not obeying the Lord in this vital area.

Jesus Christ demands a lifestyle of relationships. The whole New Testament insists that this is so. Not that it's easy . . .

> To live above with saints we love—
> O Lord, that will be glory.
> To live below with saints we know—
> Well, that's another story!

And so Ephesians 4:3 says we are to "make every effort to keep the unity of the Spirit through the bond of peace." Anyone can create an organization, but only God can create an organism. And that's what God has done in the church. Someone has said, "Anyone can count the seeds in an apple, but only God can tell how many apples are in a seed." Even so, who can measure the vast potential, resources, ramifications and future of the church as we see it? So we must love it with all our hearts.

Our relationship together is heaven-made. When you belong to Jesus, you belong to others in Jesus.

This is such a unique unity, heaven had to accomplish it. It is Christ's own work. So the Bible says that in the church we are one person, one new creation.

And we're to guard, preserve, keep the unity.

The Bible doesn't say we're to make it; Jesus has made it. It says we're to keep it. We have it—but we're to express it.

"Making every effort to keep the unity" of the church means several things. Certainly it involves working hard at communication. The goal should be that everybody understands everybody—although, obviously, in this life we'll never perfectly reach that goal!

I grew up in a Swedish-American situation, and there are lots of jokes told about the poor Swedes. One concerns a Swedish congregation that was trying to vote on the purchase of a new chandelier for the sanctuary. The haggling had gotten intense, and one old fellow had stood it as long as he could; then he rose to his feet.

"I tell you, friends," he said, "I got tree tings I vant to say to you about dis har crazy chandelier.

"In de first place, it sounds so fancy, I bet dere's not vun of you har dat could even spell *chandelier.*

"And number two, even if we had vun, dere's not anyvun har who vud know how to play it.

"And tirdly, vat dis church really needs is a good lighting fixture!"

Good communication is necessary! And yet communication is not the real key to unity in the body of Christ. Even a good secular organization can strive to achieve better communication!

What sets apart a true church—and every church leader must understand this thoroughly—is the presence of *life.* And there will never be any true unity unless there is true life.

To attempt to unify people on a theological basis, on a doctrinal creed, is absolutely a pipe dream. You've got everybody agreeing on three-and-a half years and then somebody changes his mind and thinks seven years, and everybody will be shook up—because the unity of the group is threatened.

We only have unity because we have a common life. One of the greatest hindrances to practiced unity, I suppose, is that people think they can have it by prescribing a certain polity or creed. But you only get unity of spirit by having *the* Spirit. And only Jesus ministers the Spirit to the church.

Our oneness is Christ's, not ours. We don't work it up, he sends it down. We are his, therefore we are one. He is our common life. As Ephesians 4:4 says, when we know Jesus we are a throbbing, living, vital organism. That's biblical teaching.

Then any break in fellowship, on the denominational or local or any other level, should absolutely shock us and repel us.

I remember, as a teenager playing baseball, seeing a friend

make a sudden move and throw his knee out of joint. That fellow was in such pain, he literally slithered across the grass! One of the players got a doctor, and the rest of us helped the doctor reunite the top part of his knee with the bottom part. I will never forget seeing the agony of that boy when one member of his body was out of joint with another member.

And that's how we must feel in the body of Christ! When a hurt comes, "tell it not in Gath"; don't let outsiders know. And preserve, guard, keep the unity of the Spirit! Ephesians 4:13 says to be built up "until we all reach unity in the faith."

Oh, may it become a way of life for us to enjoy that rich practice of oneness in Christ!

15.

And how do you practice unity? How do you "make every effort . . ."?

Jesus began his upper room discourse with that same call to unity. It was just before his arrest; what would be the glue that would hold together this diverse little group when he was not physically present? They differed as to temperament, politics, and personality. He said,

> A new commandment I give you: Love one another. As I have loved you, so you must love one another. All men will know that you are my disciples if you love one another (John 13:34,35).

Love is the chief mark of our authenticity. Jesus commanded believers to love each other—and what he demands of us you can be sure he also supplies to us!—"God has poured out his love into our hearts by the Holy Spirit, whom he has given us" (Rom. 5:5).

If that is so, then the Holy Spirit, our source of love, will supply all the love a Christian needs, for all the people he will ever meet, in all the situations he will ever face, for all the time he'll ever live! The unending supply of the Spirit will not fail, even in difficult times, so neither will the unending supply of love.

If you are a church leader, you have an awesome responsibility to "make every effort" to lift up the church worldwide to your people. Don't foster in your church a spirit of arrogance, or pride that you are not some other denomination—one of those awful whatevers, or members of this council or that. Don't make snide remarks about the very big churches or the very small ones, downgrading seeming successes or magnifying seeming failures. Don't gossip, don't demean, don't seek for your church "status by negation": "God, [we] thank you that [we are] not like all other men . . ." (Luke 18:11).

"Church spirit" is never built by putting others down. How strongly this strikes us when we read Christ's words to Saul when Saul thought he was only persecuting Christians: "Saul, Saul, why do you persecute *me?*" (Acts 9:4, emphasis mine). As we handle the church, so we handle Jesus Christ! When you pinch the body, the Head says, "Ouch!" When Ephesians 4:30,31 says to get rid of bitterness and slander, its literal words are, "Don't make God cry!"

Oh, love the church and speak well of her always! Praise God for the whole body of Christ and all its parts! Indeed, Calvary love in the body is seen as we "in humility consider others better than" ourselves (Phil. 2:3).

Build love in the body from the universal to the microcosmic. Teach your brothers and sisters in Christ—and model it yourself!—that the Christian home is really a mini-church. "Make every effort" for your own believing family to learn to express tenderly that implanted gift of love in outward, verbal and physical expressions of all kinds. Then it will be both "caught" and "taught" throughout the congregation.

And warm, aggressive affirmations of love must be the continual expression of your local church when the members come together. The pastor, staff and lay leaders are absolutely key here. If they "make every effort" to love each other and the people and openly to tell them so, the people will gradually learn to express love as well.

Pastor, lean over the pulpit soon and tell your congregation you love them. Even if you feel awkward, do it! They need to hear those words from you.

Opportunities in the church life for love to be expressed should be deliberately built into the program. Sometimes why not have "love feasts" before the Lord's Supper—times set aside for the honest expression of love? Especially before a Sunday evening Communion time, have your people gather in a social hall, or in nice weather on the church lawn, for a simple "stand-up" meal of bread, cheese and water. Ask them while they're eating to share with each other how they came to know Christ, or who has been a blessing in their lives, or what Christ has done for them. Encourage them to share Scripture, and to share expressions of gratitude for one another. After a good hour or so of this mingling and loving, then have them go together into the sanctuary to celebrate the Lord's Supper.

Or when the pastor has preached on love in the body of Christ, or unity, or some related theme, suggest an "appreciation time"—a time when all members, before they leave the room, find at least five people and tell them that they love them and why! Oh, how this warms up and fulfills a local church! Sometimes there are Sunday school teachers who haven't heard loving words of appreciation in years, or committee members who aren't sure they're in a particular person's good graces, or others who are simply feeling taken for granted. It's important sometimes to push your people together, to "force" them in winsome ways to get beyond the hello basis, the cups of coffee, the "hi, how are you"s. An "appreciation time" can even without suggestion become an opportunity for apologies, for mending relationships.

Understand how meshed are the three priorities—how inseparable in the heart of God. When you injure the body, you injure the Head. But as you learn to worship and lift up the

Head, lifting up the body will follow. Out of the habit of Priority One will flow the habit of Priority Two.

(And a cup of cold water to a worldling—Priority Three— is like giving it to Jesus—Priority One. *Love intertwines all the commitments.*)

Continually, then, exalt and bind together the local church. The young people must be exposed to the older, and vice versa. Ministerial students need to be related to and come under the authority of the church fathers. Everyone needs to know and enjoy and influence the boys and girls. Larger churches will have to pay particular attention to creative ways to program so that exposure to the whole spread of ages becomes a joyful and continuing experience.

And continue to stress that fundamentally your gathering is not part of an organization but an organism! If the people in your local body look at their church as an *organization,* they will see its members according to their *function*—there's George the choir director, and this is Mrs. Murphy who keeps the Sunday school attendance records. In fact, there's Charlie who doesn't teach his third grade boys *very well* . . . If they see each other according to function, to producing, then they will grade each other's performance.

If, on the other hand, they see their local church fundamentally as *an organism,* they will see the people in it as brothers and sisters, as members of the body, as what they *are* more than what they *do.* And then even the doing will be more palatable!

Through the twenty years that I was pastor of Lake Avenue Congregational Church in Pasadena, we used weekly registration cards on which people wrote messages to the pastor. Children have written me notes like these:

I like the pastors message it pleses my heat. And God bless al of you.

I hate the devil. I love the Lord. I love the pastor. I love his pritchin.

I just want you to know . . . I lik you more than penut butter sandwiches.

To this last card I wrote a thank-you note saying, "And I like you better than a hole in one."

A loving body of believers is so unique in this divided world that there can be no doubt they are God's people! It's the great mark of reality. Look once again at John 13:35: "All men will know that you are my disciples if you love one another."

Dr. Francis Schaeffer makes this powerful comment:

In the midst of the world, in the midst of our present dying culture, Jesus gives a right to the world. Upon his authority he gives the world the right to judge whether you and I are born-again Christians on the basis of our observable love toward all Christians.

That's pretty frightening. Jesus turns to the world and says, "I've got something to say to you. On the basis of my authority, I give you a right: You may judge whether or not an individual is a Christian on the basis of the love he shows to all Christians. . . ."

In other words, if people come up to us and cast in our teeth the judgment that we are not Christians because we have not shown love toward other Christians, we must understand that they are only exercising a prerogative which Jesus gave them.

And we must not get angry. If people say, "You don't love other Christians," we must go home, get down on our knees, and ask God whether or not they are right to have said what they said.

We must be very careful at this point, however. We may be true Christians, really born-again Christians, and yet fail in our love toward other Christians. As a matter of fact, to be completely realistic, it is stronger than this.

There will be times (and let us say it with tears), there will be times when we fail in our love toward each other as Christians. In a fallen world, where there is no such thing as perfection until Jesus comes, we know this will be the case. And, of course, when we fail, we must ask God's forgiveness. But Jesus is not saying that failure to love all Christians proves that we are not Christians.

Let each of us see this individually for ourselves. If I fail in my love toward Christians, it does not prove I am not a Christian. What Jesus is saying, however, is that if I do not have the love I should have toward all other Christians, the world has the right to make judgment that I am not a Christian.[25]

The world will not be impressed with the buildings or busyness of a local church, but Jesus said the world will be affected by its unity! And certainly, if the world is to become aware of it, that loving unity must be both audible and visible.

Then let the church be the church—united in love.

16.

There was a rare book collector who had a very "unbookish" friend. The friend said he had just cleaned out his ancestral attic and thrown away some old books.

"Old books?" The collector was immediately anxious. "You didn't throw away any old books—?"

"Yes," said the friend, "they were messy old things. One was a big old Bible."

"A big old Bible?" asked the collector. "What kind of big old Bible?"

"Well, it said on it Guten'—something."

"A Gutenberg Bible?" shouted the book collector. "You threw out a Gutenberg Bible? Man, do you know that that's the first book ever printed with movable type? Do you know it dates back to the fifteenth century? Do you know that one sold the other day in New York City for four million dollars?"

Said his friend, "Well, this one probably wasn't worth much. Some idiot named 'M. Luther' had scribbled stuff all through it."

It's important to learn to appreciate first things, especially in the study of the second priority, the church, the body of

Christ! It's essential to go back and back to the first church, to compare and to get corrected and adjusted.

And as we look hard at the technique for love that the New Testament teaches, we see immediately that perhaps the most effective and penetrating way for a local church to live out its loving oneness is through small groups. Love for the body of Christ cannot be a mere theoretical doctrine; it must carve out for us our very lifestyle.

The Lord Jesus loved the masses, but he gave a large proportion of his ministry to time with a selected few who loved him, believed in him and were willing to follow him. All around was the needy world, but he frequently "withdrew" (over and over in Mark's Gospel we see the word) to catch time alone with and give priority to his small group.

In the personal lifestyle of our Savior we see his three priorities at work. He often withdrew totally for his first commitment of giving his attention to his Father. Second, he deliberately gave much time to his inner circle of disciples. And third, he gave himself in preaching and healing to the world at large.

Then the great emphasis of the New Testament epistles is for us to do the same: to love the Lord and to give ourselves generously to each other, building up and caring for each other, in order to be ready to minister to the needs of the world at large. The last phrase of Galatians 6:10 spells out this special priority of God's family: "Therefore, as we have opportunity, let us do good to all people, especially to those who belong to the family of believers." Fellow believers are to have a higher priority than those outside of Christ.

The apostle Paul modeled the same priorities. And he always had around him a small group of encouraging, ministering brothers. He even included them when he wrote letters: "Paul and Timothy, servants of Christ Jesus . . ." (to the Philippians); "Paul, Silas and Timothy . . ." (to the Thessalonians); "Paul . . . and Timothy our brother . . ." (to the Colossians).

And both the Lord Jesus and the apostle Paul were careful to say as they were leaving this life, "Now, don't be the end of the line! You turn around and do what I have done." Said Jesus, "Go make disciples, teaching them everything I've taught you . . ." (Matt. 28:18–20). Said Paul, "The things you have heard me say . . . entrust to reliable men who will also be qualified to teach others" (2 Tim. 2:2). In other words, "Keep the chain of discipling going!"

Incidentally, when we say "small group" we really mean *small*: not fifteen or twenty but between four and eight believers together. (Wesley said between five and ten.) Now it's true that Jesus had twelve, larger than we have found practical. But for those men, at least during the last year and a half of Jesus' ministry, their togetherness was a full-time occupation. In our lifestyle today, we have found through trial and error that if groups get larger than eight, someone starts being neglected.[26]

The pattern in the New Testament is for the loving family of believers to disciple each other. Acts 2:46,47 describes the early church in the first fullness of the Holy Spirit, and before persecution began, as functioning daily in two places: in the temple courts and in homes.

So must the people in a local body! They must move into each other's lives, in honor prefer one another, edify one another, admonish and instruct one another, greet one another with a holy kiss, care for one another, serve one another, be honest with (lie not to) one another, comfort one another, and James adds, "confess [their] sins to each other"(see James 5:16). That all takes close relationships, and it means spending much time together.

If Matthew 28:19 says that all of us are to make disciples, this implies intimate contact and personal influence but not the same prescribed method for every Christian. Discipling is not necessarily meeting weekly to fill in blanks in study books; it's life rubbing against life toward the end of producing mature believers. In this loose, general sense, every Christian must be taught to feel responsible for discipling—for influencing other believers around him toward maturity.

Church leaders must be particularly conscious of leading their people into a balanced lifestyle. There are three usual levels of contact among the people of our churches, and these three levels each need to be strong and in balance with the other.

Peter Wagner begins each of these levels with a *c:* "celebration," "congregation," and "cell." The "celebration" is the worship service, usually once a week, which can have in it any number, from two to thousands. The point of worship is not interpersonal relationships, but believers gathered one-on-one before God. If we try to make this service a horizontal fellowship time, the larger the church grows the more disappointing the experience will be. The "celebration" must strongly connect each worshiper with God himself.

The "congregation" in a small church involves the same people as the worship service, but it performs a different function. A "congregation's" size can vary from 25 to 175 members, and it's the place where a person can have a sense of belonging, of being known and cared for. Once Sunday morning attendance grows past 175, adult Sunday school classes must become the "congregations," where not only Bible teaching goes on but casseroles are sent to the sick, "heart lines" are mobilized for emergency prayer, and all kinds of socializing binds the groups together.

But when a church stops there and does not strongly encourage the third level, the "cell," that church gets full of bottled-up people who have no place to express their joys and sorrows and get help. The largest, most expensive counseling staff will not suffice; many people won't go. But when people worship God in the "celebration," socialize in a "congregation," and express their needs and fears and victories in a "cell"—learning more of God's Word at all three levels—their lives have every chance of being whole and satisfied.

There was a time when our pastoral team of thirteen was having its weekly meeting, and one of the pastors said, "By the way, who's doing all the counseling these days? My counseling load has gone down to a third or a half of what it used to be." The fellows all looked around at each other and discovered that *all* their counseling loads had shrunk. When we probed to see when this began to happen, we discovered it was several years before, when the practice of meeting in small groups had been instigated! Problems were getting nipped in the bud week by week, and the body in general had risen to a new level of health.

Now when this kind of truth dawns on a church, the leaders are apt to say, "Wonderful! Let's train some leadership and divide up our whole congregation into small groups!"

Immediately they're off to at best a shaky start. The more heavily small groups are administrated from above, the more cumbersome the operation for the church and the more dissatisfied the people! If specific rules had been necessary, the New Testament epistles would have surely laid them out for us.

Some warnings are in order: it's important for church leaders not to be heavy-handed with small groups. Don't keep a tight rein. Don't divide up the alphabet ("all of the *A*'s through *C*'s together, all the *D*'s through *F*'s . . .") Don't slice up the people by neighborhoods. (To one of the most exciting groups Anne and I have ever been in, the members traveled an average of thirty miles!) Let there be no artificial groupings.

Small groups at their best are grassroots movements. As the church leaders strongly preach them, teach them, and model them, small groups will sprout up by the promptings of the Holy Spirit. Let the people find each other—probably best friends with best friends until they're comfortable. Just teach them to decide on cut-off times so that the groups will multiply by dividing!

There is usually no need for church leaders to train small group leadership or to tell them what to "study." Small groups are not primarily for the purpose of study, anyway. We suggest five ingredients for small groups:
1. Worship
2. The Word
3. Sharing
4. Prayer
5. Accountability.

Following these simple guidelines, sometimes neighbors will join together, sometimes old may join with young, rich may join with poor, parents may join with their teenagers or even younger children. Some of the groups will be true discipling groups, in which case their leader will certainly want to pick his or her own agenda. Some of the groups will be supportive fellowships for peers—perhaps for singles, perhaps for couples, and hopefully at least some with singles and couples together. These support groups can pick their own leaders or maybe rotate the leadership.[27]

Some groups will be heavily into teaching and learning. Some will emphasize sharing. Some will build in local evangelistic projects or missionary projects or social times. Church leaders can gently guide with the suggestion of the "five ingredients," but it's best to let the proportions come as they will, and the Holy Spirit will cause all kinds of creativity to bubble up, with both depth and fun, laughter and tears, built in.

Just as no two individual Christians are alike, no two small groups will ever come out alike. But the more creative ones will become pacesetters, and before long groups will copy each other, or occasionally mix—or only the Lord knows what.

17.

Gilbert Tennant (1703–1764), one of the great preachers of his day, pastored a Presbyterian church in Philadelphia during the Great Awakening of the eighteenth century. His church was even made up of converts from that great revival. At one time he preached a sermon called "Brotherly Love Recommended by the Argument of the Love of Christ." In it he urged his congregation to love each other, and to love each other to the end. Tennant made the important observation that when Christians move close to each other, they get to know each other's faults. It is at this crucial point that they must press in more, through pain and self-discipline, to perfect their love for each other until they have a deep, settled, and secure love which continues in spite of everything!

The results of that Great Awakening were conserved by gathering believers into small groups for discipling. John and Charles Wesley, working in England about the same time Tennant was preaching in America, called them "class meetings," or "little societies," and it was this "method" of small groups which became "Methodism," the most powerful spiritual force of its day.

Peter Bohler was a Moravian pastor who was used by God in the conversion of John Wesley, and who was a great influence in Wesley's life and ministry. Together these zealots for the Lord published a paper which is quoted here in part:

Orders of a Religious Society Meeting in Fetter's Lane, in obedience to the command of God by St. James, and by the advice of Peter Bohler, May 1, 1738, it was agreed,

1. That they will meet together once in a week to confess their faults one to another, and pray for one another that they may be healed.

2. That any others, of whose Sincerity they are well assured, may, if they desire it, meet with them for that Purpose. And, May 29, it was agreed,

3. That the Persons desirous to meet together for that Purpose, be divided into several Bands, or little Societies;

4. That none of these consist of fewer than five or more than ten Persons.

5. That some Person in each Band be desired to interrogate the rest in order, who may be called the Leader of that Band. And on Monday, September 26, it was agreed,

6. That each Band meet twice in a week, once on Monday evenings, the second Time when it is most convenient for each Band.

7. That every Person come punctually at the Hour appointed, without some extraordinary Reason.

8. That those that are present begin exactly at the Hour.

9. That every Meeting be begun and ended with Singing and Prayer.

10. That every one in order speak as freely, plainly, and concisely as he can, the real State of his Heart, with his several Temptations and Deliverances, since the last Time of meeting . . .[28]

There were several dozen more rules! I have to believe that the power in these thousands of tight little groups was not in their rules, but in the fact that each member was required to reveal "the real State of his Heart." This is courageous Christianity at its best!

18.

Christianity, when it is honest, open and loving at intimate levels, powerfully changes individual and collective human behavior.

Bruce Larson says this, and it has been quoted by many people:

> The neighborhood bar is possibly the best counterfeit there is to the fellowship Christ wants to give His church. It's an imitation—dispensing liquor instead of grace, escape rather than reality, but it is a permissive, accepting and inclusive fellowship. It is unshockable. It is democratic. You can tell people secrets and they usually don't tell others or even want to.
>
> The bar flourishes, not because most people are alcoholics, but because God has put into the human heart the desire to know and be known, to love and be loved. And so many seek a counterfeit at the price of a few beers.
>
> Christ wants his church to be unshockable, democratic, permissive—a fellowship where people can come in and say, "I'm sunk!" "I'm beat!" "I've had it!" Alcoholics Anonymous has this quality. Our churches too often miss it.

Any local church is a gathering of people with many, many wounds. They come out of a world where they've been beaten up from one week to the next. They need grace and love and tender handling, and they need it from each other.

Small groups give us the perfect opportunity to be "unshockable, democratic, permissive"—to be comforting, to be "shock-absorbers." But more than that is needed. Christians who are unshockable and loving are the only ones qualified to also be corrective.

You remember how Paul in Galatians 2 withstood Peter to his face; he "bawled him out" in front of other believers! You would think that Peter would have said, "Well, that's enough. Never again am I going to get close to that fellow Paul. I'll never forget how he treated me; I was so embarrassed."

But when Peter closed his second book he said, "Oh, yes, and there's our beloved brother Paul . . ." He understood "tough love," and he loved Paul in return for the love Paul had for him—love which was committed enough to correct.

On the other hand, Paul in 1 Corinthians 15 wrote about those who had had a special experience with Christ after his resurrection and he particularly singled out Peter: "he was seen of Cephas." He gave Cephas, or Peter, special recognition—a special, high place of honor—in his witness to the resurrection. No rebuke on Paul's part could detract from the high regard he gave to this great Christian leader.

Christians going through temptations and difficult times especially need the loving closeness of a few brothers and sisters who will hold them accountable.

One brother, just out of the drug scene, came into a group of which I was a member. He was living with his girlfriend. The other members of the group found out about it and held him fast in love, but they gave him nothing but trouble over it! I remember one morning in the church parking lot, as we were parting and moving farther and farther from each other, one of the fellows continued to call, "Kick her out! Kick her out! Kick her out!"

For months he struggled; eventually his brothers prayed and loved him into victory in the situation. Today he is married to a wonderful girl and is in a strategic, full-time Christian ministry.

Part B:

The second priority in the private life of a church leader

19.

How important it is for Christian leaders not just to talk but to do! How important it is for the lives they model to be consistent with the Scriptures they so fervently espouse!

Jesus ministered to the masses—but he gave much of his time privately to the Twelve, and out of the Twelve he seemed to give particular attention to an inner circle of three. Then in the book of Acts it was not young men emerging from those masses who took leadership in the new church—it was the Twelve, and out of the Twelve particularly Peter, James, and John, the three to whom Jesus had given the most intimate attention.

How did Jesus disciple this select group of men? Again and again, as we see in the Gospels, he withdrew from the crowds to spend time with his inner circle. (The greatest gift one person can give another is time!)

Mark 3:7: "Jesus withdrew with his disciples . . ."

Mark 3:13: "Jesus went up into the hills and called to him those he wanted . . ."

Mark 7:17: "After he had left the crowd and entered the house, his disciples asked him about this parable . . ."

Mark 9:28: "After Jesus had gone indoors, his disciples asked him privately . . ."

Mark 9:33: "When he was in the house, he asked them . . ."

Following Jesus' example, Christian leaders will see their ministries endure in direct proportion to the quality time they have poured into an inner circle of disciples. Think of Miss Henrietta Mears. In earlier decades she was a dynamic leader of Christian education at the First Presbyterian Church of Hollywood. But the young men she discipled (some even living in her home) have multiplied her ministry many times over: Bill Bright, Dick Halverson, Louis Evans, Jr., Don Moomaw, Don and Ted Cole, Bob Munger, and many others.

I am convinced that the effective pastor, professor, counselor, Christian administrator is also to be a Christlike discipler. His or her life, faith, love for God—even through struggles and weaknesses—must be constantly rubbing off on hand-picked people close to him, people who will in turn influence others.

When I was serving as senior pastor in a church, I felt I had three primary responsibilities: to preach, to administrate, and to disciple small groups. And I insisted that each member of the staff, whatever his or her other duties, be committed to discipling his own family and also other small groups. It was one way that the philosophy of ministry of the three priorities was consistent throughout the church—it began with 100 percent of the leadership.

Now, of course, *discipling* is a general term which has many levels of meaning. Preaching the Word on Sundays, Sunday school teaching, Bible class teaching—these are certainly forms of discipling, but not at a very intimate level. Pastors, staffers, church leaders need to give themselves to ministering to the large crowds if they have the gifts to do so—but no one should be exempt from discipling small groups. Only as leaders set the example can they expect the church members to follow.

How wonderful it is when Christian leaders see their families as their primary disciples, their closest, most intimate small group! How rich family life will become when this is true!

If a Christian husband sees his wife and children as just his wife and children, he'll treat them as any worldling does: he'll see that they're properly clothed and schooled, marry well . . .

But if a Christian husband sees his wife and children as his chief responsibility among those he is discipling, he will realize he has a limited period of time (perhaps twenty years with each child) in which to live intimately and well before them and so to reproduce godliness in the next generation. Then he will carry out Matthew 28:19 in their lives, seeing that they are baptized and teaching them everything Jesus has taught him. Seen in this light, family devotions will take on fresh motivation. Teaching loved ones to tithe, worship, have their own quiet times, witness to the unsaved—everything will become part of the total picture of discipling. And commitment and perseverance learned within this special inner circle when things are rough will carry over into the larger circle—the church as a whole—when things get rough there!

But discipling for Christian leaders shouldn't stop with their own families. It's also important for them to take the lead in discipling small groups outside the family circle. Small groups of this kind are where interactions will most expose, prayers will most strengthen, and encouraging love will most comfort and edify. In small groups Christianity is seen in living color!

My own life was enriched and deeply changed when I began to meet with my first small group of men (see 2 Tim. 2:2). I had always had groups around me; but some years ago, as we were seeking to take more seriously the models of Christ and the apostle Paul, I realized my great need to be obedient to the biblical pattern.

I called in a few close brothers. I also called in my wife and my secretary; this was so important to me, I wanted them to be witnesses!

"Guys," I said, "I've had it. I'm exhausted, and I think I'm exhausted because I haven't been ministering in a specifically biblical method. I see that Jesus worked through a small band of men, and for at least a year I'd like you fellows to become that. I'd like two hours a week of your time."

Well, they all with one accord began to make excuses! They were really busy men, and I understood that. Making that kind of commitment was going to take real sacrifice.

Finally one of them said, "Fellows, this is not a discussion time. This is an altar call!" And he went from one to another saying, "Will you? Will you?" They all said yes, and that year with those beautiful brothers became a revolutionary new beginning in my personal life. I learned that I could never again live without the body of Christ with me at deep levels, at biblical close range!

Through the years since, I've never been without support groups of peers, where I was one among others (sometimes with Anne in mixed groups of couples and singles), and I've never been without discipling groups where I've assumed a more direct leadership role. A few years ago I asked God for the privilege of discipling a hundred young men, and God has honored that request.

On rare occasions I've used a Moses-and-Joshua type of discipling, one-on-one. But the greatest joy has been discipling small groups of fellows, as Jesus did and as Paul did—most often early in the morning. Out of these rich times have come church leadership and also young pastors and churches around the world.

When Jesus chose his group he selected them with great care:

> One of those days Jesus went out into the hills to pray, and spent the night praying to God. When morning came, he called his disciples to him and chose twelve of them . . . (Luke 6:12,13).

I believe that the Father gave the Son those twelve names during that important night of prayer. Later, in his prayer to the Father recorded in John 17 he called them the men "whom you gave me out of the world."

Any Christian leader must select with prayer those with

whom he'd spend quality time discipling. Jesus' twelve seemed to have three special qualifications: availability, teachability, and a certain heart for God. Sometimes I haven't chosen my small groups well, and then I've reaped the results of wrong choices! If Jesus chose those men only after much prayer, the modern discipler should do the same.

Jesus concentrated on a few, selected them carefully, and built them together into a loving unity.[29] When he commanded his disciples in John 13:34 to love one another in the same way that he himself loved them, they could understand very well all the patience, care and commitment he expected to be involved! The "bottom line" of discipling is love, and small groups are God's perfect laboratory for working out that love in everyday relationships.

If the body of Christ is indeed our second priority, then the ministry of loving and discipling must be entered into wholeheartedly by both church leaders and people. I myself cannot overestimate how powerfully this has facilitated my own ministry. Men at close range have helped me through my times of deepest need, and I know I have grown in Christ as I have entered into the joy of discipling.

There are guidelines that we've used together that have been helpful:

1. Form groups of from four to eight.

2. Make sure it is clear that this is a genuine commitment and that attendance will be regular. Make a contract!

3. Agree from the beginning on the meeting times, on how long the meetings will be, and on your final meeting date— probably in six months to a year. Cut-off times give importance to the period of time you're together! Of course, a group may agree later to an extension.

4. When the group is finished, the understanding is that each member will go on to disciple others.

For myself, I've picked scriptures and projects that serve as curriculum and ministry together, and all that Anne and I have learned together about specific techniques for discipling are in her book, *Discipling One Another.*[30]

20.

A member of our small group joined the rest of us one morning complaining loudly. (He's a person who just lives life in living color.)

"What's the matter with you, Dave?" we asked.

"I'm burnt!" said Dave. "It's our wedding anniversary today, and we're so broke I can't even take Mary out to dinner."

We had a wonderful time together that morning, especially praying for Dave's and Mary's marriage and their life and ministry together. And when Dave left, somehow a wad of dollar bills had found their way into his pocket from the brothers, so he could go celebrate with Mary.

A few months later Dave arrived at the group in a mood of high joy. (Dave's lows and his highs were always both loud, both obvious to all.)

He slapped four thousand dollars down on the coffee table in front of us. "Guys," said Dave, "I just sold a little building and this is my tithe, and you fellows have to help me spend it quick before I gobble it up for other things."

What fun we had that morning! Each of us knew of specific Christian needs, mostly missionary needs, and we had a great time spending four thousand dollars of the Lord's money.

Small groups are full of serendipities. They keep the Christian leader in touch with flesh-and-blood humanity, and they force him to be a "real person" himself!

A wonderful couple once came to our church when the husband joined the staff of a Christian organization nearby. Until then he'd pastored churches, and for a couple of years he was like a fish out of water without a congregation!

"Herb," I kept telling him, "you need a small group around you to supply that need for close relationships."

"Ray," he kept answering, "groups like that are just a lot of hot air being blown around—the blind leading the blind!"

But after a while he began to meet with a breakfast group of five or six godly businessmen.

Eventually Herb was transferred in his ministry to another state, and before he left he said to me, "Ray, I can leave California, though I love it. I can even leave this wonderful church. But what's driving me crazy is leaving those six guys in my small group. They mean so much to me. They have stretched me and made me a more open, growing person than I've ever been. How I love them!"

"But," he added, "when I move, my first business is to pray for another group."

Whatever you do in life, don't do it solo! Do it in company with brothers and sisters in Christ! It's the New Testament pattern, and it's what keeps the body of Christ whole and loving and self-corrective.

Are you a teacher? You dare not teach alone. You need those around you who are ministering to you, so that you teach in fellowship with others. They know what you're teaching; they know what you're saying. They know your difficulties; they know about that special student who needs particular love and understanding.

Are you a preacher? Acts 2:14 says that "Peter stood up with the Eleven, raised his voice and addressed the crowd." I used to scratch my head wondering how Peter could preach "with the Eleven."

I already had formulated in my philosophy that my preaching was not a single voice, that I had no right to say whatever I pleased. My preaching had to be the united "halleluia" of the entire church. I was not only speaking *to* them but *for* them, on their behalf, correctly reflecting their doctrines and their views.

But practically, how could I preach "with the Eleven"— with special, committed brothers and sisters? I decided at least I could ask volunteers to meet in a side room of the sanctuary and pray for me all the time I was preaching. We chose a little room where the sound of the service was piped in, so they would know what was happening though the volume was turned low. And they prayed through the whole service:

"Lord, bless the organist right now during the prelude . . ."

"Lord, help the first-timers to feel welcome and at ease . . ."

"Now make the words of this first hymn come alive . . ."

And throughout the sermon I knew I was being constantly supported in prayer.

Then I discovered—no wonder Charles Spurgeon was one of the great preachers of the English-speaking world! Every time he preached there were five hundred in the basement praying for him!

Christian leader or church staffer, when you go to work, does anyone really know about your needs, so that he is prayerfully attending to you while you're at work? Are there a few brothers or sisters in a group who are supporting you while you do what you do? Wouldn't it be great if there were no business people in your church who ever went to their jobs without knowing that someone that day was saying, "Lord, bless my friend; I know he needs special help right now with this interview or with this job he's doing, or this person he's working with; Lord, be near him"? And each one, then, is being supplied, is being ministered to, is able to work properly because of the ministry of a brother or a sister.

I know many small groups who exchange their fresh schedules every week in pairs, so that two by two they can pray each other through their specific activities of that week. So

the body of Christ learns to feel responsible for each other—
and accountable to each other.

The reason that when I go to speak in conferences I go in
teams and never alone is that I feel I must operate within
the framework of the body of Christ. There will be little power
when I "fly solo"; in the New Testament it just isn't done.
(Exception: Philip, in Acts 8, fleeing alone from persecution,
successfully ministered to the Samaritans as he ran—but the
apostles back in Jerusalem quickly shored him up with Peter
and John to be his team.)

This is what we have in 1 Corinthians 12 when Paul says,
"Look, the ear cannot say, because it is not the eye, 'Well,
I'm much less effective than the eye, you don't need me!' Nor
can the hand say to the foot, 'I'm far more dexterous than
you; I don't need you!' No, no," says Paul, "everybody needs
everybody! No inferiority, no superiority in the body. We all
belong to each other; we all need each other; we must all
work together" (author's paraphrase).

Christian leader, you have a special problem. (I could never
say this if I were not your brother in this situation.) The ten-
dency is for you to come into the body of Christ willing to
help—but never to unmask enough to be helped! "Big" Christians (by "big" Christians I mean those who have big responsibilities and are looked up to—"big wheels") tend to operate
in the body at the advisory level. In that way they're saying,
"I don't need you, but you very much need me." Pastors and
other Christian leaders can easily fall into the trap of functioning by always teaching other Christians what to do!

Keep your relationships in the body two-way. Let others
minister to you. Be willing to be ministered to. Are you always
on the side of correction, or do you allow a brother to correct
you? Oh, it's very important in the body of Christ that we
not only give advice, but that we also ask for it.

In my discipling groups I must do this—but this is also
why I feel it important to include in my life at least one support
group of which *I am not the leader.* Even in my pastoring
years I was careful to do this—to be in at least one group

with my parishioners where I was just a member of the group—
not only leading but being led, exposing my needs as well as
my knowledge. This is so important!

John Calvin said this:

> No member of the body of Christ is endowed with such perfec-
> tion as to be able, without the assistance of others, to supply his
> own necessities!

No wonder God's Holy Spirit, the great Administrator of
the church, determined for believers to function perhaps in
large groups, but certainly in small ones:

> It is no exaggeration to say that Christ's decision to select the
> Twelve was one of the most crucial decisions of the world. There
> is no reason to suppose that we should ever have heard of the
> gospel apart from this carefully conceived step. . . .
> Since Christ wrote no book, he depended entirely upon the faith-
> fulness of the prepared group. Not all of them proved faithful,
> yet in the end, the method succeeded. The precious existence of
> the church is evidence that the method was fundamentally sound.[31]

Oneness in the body of Christ is God-made. In a real sense
it's "out of this world." It's unity based on the mystery of
the glorious unity of the Father with his Son (see John 17:22).

In the nitty-gritty give-and-take of small groups, in the inter-
action of God with his people at close range, we learn that
we are truly members one of another; we learn to act out
this unity; we learn to visibly and audibly love each other,
to break down those barriers of pain and by the grace of Christ
to fight our way to each other.

Sometimes I've known it to take the physical act of getting
down on our knees to pray to bring some of us to humility
and oneness.

And at that point there was added the glory of God!

Section Three
OUR THIRD PRIORITY—

THE WORLD

Part A:
The third priority in the public life of a church

21.

This is a true story. In a famous, historic church in the heart of a busy city, there is at the front an enormous painting of our crucified Savior.

Three people one day came in singly, in silence, to pray. First an old man walked slowly in, sat down on a front pew, and began to gaze at the beautiful picture of Christ. He did not notice a woman who came in behind him and sat down in silence. Nor did either see the young girl who slipped in behind them.

As they sat there unconscious of each other, the old man in rapture finally spoke out loud: "Bless him; I love him." Without moving her eyes the woman said, "I love him, too." And the girl added, "So do I."

There, in the heart of a bustling world, three believers sat adoring the Lord Jesus. And somehow between them there was a quiet bond of love and appreciation for each other.

But what none of the three realized was that around the top of the old sanctuary was a gallery for tourists, and they were being silently observed.

"Oh," came from one tourist in a choked murmur, "I'd like to know what they know."

And another tourist added, ". . . and love as they love . . ."

Three priorities, three commitments, three loves. Attachment to our great God and Savior Jesus Christ must effect an attachment to each other in the body of Christ. And that close, loving bond to each other will have its effect on the world.

Remember the logical order in John 15:

"Abide in me" (v. 4, KJV),

"Love one another" (v. 12, KJV),

"Go and bring forth fruit" (v. 16, KJV).

The priorities must be kept in that order: one, two, three. Spelling out the order is simple enough, but kneading them deeply into the total "stuff" of our devotions and our lifestyles takes a whole lifetime to accomplish, and takes much concentration in a local church.

Out of commitment to Christ must flow our commitment to each other in his body. Only when we are rich in him and in his Word will we richly feed and nourish one another.

And out of our commitment to each other must flow our commitment to the world. None of this mindset of "God-bless-us-four-no-more" exclusivism, as somebody expressed in this tart little poem:

> We are God's chosen few;
> All the rest are damned.
> There's no room in heaven for you;
> We don't want heaven crammed!

No, together—in teams, in cooperation, in strategy, through prayer and maybe through tears—we must reach and reach and reach.

22.

You know the slogan from "Peanuts": "Today the neighborhood, tomorrow the world!" Every church must reach to its neighborhood, and reach to the world.

Mark 2:1–12 gives us a vivid picture of how the second priority facilitates the third priority in evangelism of the neighborhood and the local community—how love between believers will help get new ones to Christ.

You know the story well: four men carried a paralytic to the Lord, who was so surrounded by crowds in a home that they let the cripple down through the roof, and Jesus healed him.

I see three crucial lessons for us here.

First, *unity among believers brings people to Jesus.* There lay a man—paralyzed physically, just as unbelievers in your community are paralyzed morally and spiritually.

Jenny, a non-Christian friend of ours, seemed lifted in her spirits a couple of months ago.

"I feel so much better!" she said. "I'm not smoking and drinking anymore. I'm really getting in shape, and I'm sleeping and eating better too."

"You're not smoking anymore!" we said. "Wonderful!"

"Absolutely!" she glowed. "Just one little cigarette a day to reward myself for being such a good girl."

"Oh, oh . . ." we thought. Within a few weeks she was smoking again a lot—and saying things like, "Nobody asked me out last night, so I just had some fun with a few cocktails all by myself and reading a good book . . ."

The poet Ovid described such people this way:

> I see the right, approve it too,
> Condemn the wrong—yet wrong pursue.

They're paralyzed!

So four believers in Jesus cooperated to bring this particular paralytic to him.

You know, Christians stimulate each other. They are willing to do with others what they'd never attempt alone. A fellow in a small group with me once said about this passage, "I'm the fourth man here who put his hand to the stretcher. I'm not the kind who leads boldly in initiating things, but I love to be with the guys who do!"

One man in this story in Mark's Gospel had to get the idea: "Fellows, there's poor old Joe over there. Why don't we carry him together to Jesus? Something's sure to happen if we do." So he enlisted the other three.

It took unity to get him there—but unity is costly. What if three wanted to carry him slowly, and the fourth one was frisky and wanted to dogtrot all the way? Old Joe would have ended up on the ground. Or what if they came to a tree, and two wanted to go left and two wanted to go right?

Cooperating means submission, sometimes swallowing your opinions; it means fitting in with the rest; it means love in action.

People, even Christian people, can be great individualists. "No one's going to tell *me* what to do!" More than just hacking to pieces the precious unity of the church, this spirit can keep Christians who have it from helping paralyzed people get to Christ. Isolated believers just aren't attractive.

Evangelism—loving people to Christ—calls for teamwork! How Jesus and his disciples worked together! He sent out his disciples two by two. Paul and company went everywhere together. Today, small Bible study groups, supporting one another and praying for one another as they seek to love that one or this one, can be most effective in reaching our "neighborhood-world" for Christ.

Read again Mark 2:2. When the people heard that Jesus had come home, "so many gathered that there was no room left, not even outside the door, and he preached the word to them." To go with Christ is costly. Where Jesus is, needy people keep coming, jostling, pressing in on the situation. There's confusion, there's the draining of emotions. It's costly to get into the business of loving, helping, restoring, healing, caring!

But the effect on the world may be powerful. Jesus prayed later "that all of [my followers] may be one, Father . . . *that the world may believe . . .*" (John 17:21). Then he prayed, "May they be brought to complete unity *to let the world know* . . ." (v. 23). Christian unity brings people to Jesus! And Jesus had already told the disciples, *"All men will know* that you are my disciples if you love one another" (John 13:35).

Small groups are perfect little laboratories for testing and proving that Christian unity brings people to Jesus. Anne and I were quite a while in a group with four other couples who met each Thursday evening of the month, except the third Thursday when the group together hosted a special Bible study for our unsaved friends. We met in each other's living rooms, put on a nice spread of refreshments as "bait," and conducted a low-key, hang-loose discussion of some evangelistic passage of Scripture. Loving cooperation and lots of prayer behind the scenes on the part of those couples proved that God's principle works: dozens of friends came to accept Christ in that Bible study!

Encourage your small groups to put all three priorities to practice within their groups: they must spend some time together worshiping the Lord; they must pray for and care for each other; and they must have some project together to do exploits for God.

Second, bold ingenuity brings people to Jesus. Mark 2:4 reads,

> Since they could not get him to Jesus because of the crowd, they made an opening in the roof above Jesus and, after digging through it, lowered the mat the paralyzed man was lying on.

Don't think for a minute that in biblical times it was common practice to break up somebody's roof! It was bold; it was shocking! Only desperation would make these men do such a thing. Luke mentions that they took the tiles out first, and Mark goes on to say they dug away at the mud under the tiles. The four just didn't give up!

Many believers are willing to make some effort at soul-winning; they may invite someone to a meeting or two and perhaps feed him a meal. But if an obstacle comes they quickly give up: "I did what I could; it just isn't the right time yet . . ." Or "I planted, maybe another will reap . . ." We give up so quickly—especially if we're all alone in the project!

These men probably had a strategy session. "What are we going to do with old Joe? He can't help himself; Jesus is his only answer."

"But that place is packed! They'll never let us in!"

Creative idea number one had been "Let's carry old Joe to Jesus."

Now comes creative idea number two: "Let's try the outside stairs. Maybe there's a window somewhere."

No window. "All right, what's next?"

"Man, he's right underneath us. For Joe's sake there's got to be a way. Fellows, what if we . . ."

"You're kidding. You wouldn't . . ."

And creative idea number three is born: "Guys, this is an emergency. Start digging!"

Consider carefully, and understand: when Christians realize how wonderful God is, how long eternity is, and how hot hell is—*they'll start digging.* They'll use their sanctified ingenuity!

Every family ought to strategize how to get people to Jesus. Every small group ought to strategize, and so should every Sunday school class, every church—in more creative ways than ever. There should be new churches, new Christians. Any and every effort is worth it! And *love will find ways!*

Nonconventional approaches are needed. We're apt to make fun when we see "Jesus saves" painted on a rock. But the fact is, *he does*—and some passing truck driver might be desperate enough to read, believe, and have his life changed. Cynicism over methods is a "cop-out."

Someone said to Dwight Moody, "I don't like your method of evangelism."

"Neither do I, sometimes," said Moody. "What's yours?"

"I don't have any," was the answer.

Said Moody, "I like mine better than yours."

Mark 2 offers glorious proof that the end may justify the means. Traditions must never be dearer to us than people! I'm not necessarily advocating painting on rocks, but I believe a sophisticated, superior attitude is worse.

Verse 12 of that chapter paraphrased is the comment of the onlookers: "Well, I've seen everything now!" By their attitudes they might have been saying, "We don't want anyone to come to Jesus who doesn't come by the front door. And quietly, please!" Run-of-the-mill preaching has been described as a mild-mannered preacher telling mild-mannered people to be more mild-mannered!

When a local church is falling into decay and death, the "seven last words" of the people will probably be, "We've never done it that way before."

Probably all some of those people ever saw was the hole in the roof. They didn't really see Jesus. They didn't see a man healed of his sins and his sickness. They didn't notice miracles. "Wasn't it terrible how those men tore up the roof?"

Too many times we've said, "I want people to find Christ—but please keep all the hymn tunes from the period before

1900." Friend, we've got to be willing to get holes in our roof! We've got to do whatever we can to break the stalemates, the barriers that keep our community paralytics from our Christ!

The third lesson that I see from Mark 2:1–12: *faith brings people to Jesus.* Verse 5 says that "when Jesus saw their faith, he said to the paralytic, 'Son, your sins are forgiven.' "

Whose faith? *Their* faith. This story doesn't exclude the faith of the paralytic, but it concentrates on the faith of the four who brought him. *They believed Jesus would use their efforts.* And that made carrying the dead weight of a grown man through the streets and up the stairs and through a hole in the roof—all that—worth it.

Others were perhaps saying, "What a sideshow!" Faith acts. Unbelief only reacts.

Many Christians haven't led anyone to Christ—ever—or not for so many years that they really don't think God would ever use them in this way! To overcome their dullness, their lack of hope—to build faith—they need to team up with believers who believe!

> You'll do more
> When you're four
> Than you've ever done
> When you're one!

The story ends with everyone around Jesus being amazed. The healed man was amazed. The four who carried him were amazed. The whole crowd was amazed.

And that's what life in the church will be when brothers and sisters in Christ believe deeply in the power of their common Lord as their first priority, and when they commit themselves to live and love together as their second priority, and when they move out in unity and innovation and faith to the needy world around them as their third priority.

Then church life will be amazing and wonderful to behold!

23.

There are at least five ways that every local church, while working out these three priorities, should grow.

1. The healthy church must grow numerically as well as spiritually.

2. The healthy church must grow far from its home base through world missions.

3. The healthy church must plant new churches nearby.

4. The healthy church must encourage the existing churches around it.

5. The healthy church must work in social concern within its own community.

Let's examine each of these methods for growth.

It's extremely important for pastor and staff and church leaders to make courageous plans for local evangelism. And this evangelism must be culturally acceptable. Too often the local church is not sensitive to its own community, and it either offends the people around it or misses them altogether.

Our Lord went out in real life with the people—eating and drinking with them and attending their parties. He was with the hungry, the sick, the proud, the street women, the rich, the five-times-divorced. Church leaders must find the acceptable avenues over which the gospel can travel in their area to get a fair hearing.

Some churches really profit from door-to-door, "cold turkey" visitation, or even street meetings. Some churches lure their community through Christian concerts and plays.

I've pastored churches that did all of these—and that had Evangelism Explosion teams, friendship evangelism dinners, and home desserts where testimonies were given and the gospel presented; Jewish dinners with Hebrew speakers for the Jewish friends of the community; Sunday evening "Guestevents" in which evangelistic messages were specifically preached and testimonies given; women's luncheons with evangelistic speakers; ice cream socials on the church lawn to lure in the neighbors; weekly newspaper columns and radio "shorts" targeted for nonbelievers; open-line telephone messages taped daily, with counselors there to talk over problems . . . Team efforts are without number once the creative juices start flowing.

But whatever the methods, follow-through must be built in so that new Christians can be folded into the life of the church for nurturing. To get visitors or even decisions only, and not to make disciples, is a tragic mistake.

On the New Year's Eve which ushered in Lake Avenue Church's seventy-fifth anniversary year, during a time of sharing together, one of the pastors said, "The number 7-5-0 keeps coming to my mind. Why don't we record all those each of us leads to Christ this seventy-fifth year, and ask the Lord for 750?"

At the end of that year the actual number of decisions reported was 930! And yet there were few new people in the church as a result. The church had given too much emphasis to decisions and too little to discipling. Of course it was a great goal, but we learned we must also have a strategy of incorporation.

Jesus commanded his disciples, when he left them, to turn around and make their own disciples—by going, baptizing, and teaching (Matt. 28:18–20). The process of folding the new lambs into the sheepfold must be carefully worked out. The pastoral staffs of the churches I've served each learned that they had to have a thought-through process of folding in order to conserve the results of evangelism and to build new believers into their fellowships.

Here are the six steps of the process as worked out by the staff of one of these churches:

Step One. Visitors attending all church services, musicals, and other occasions, as they were being welcomed, were asked to fill out registration cards.

Step Two. The next week a home call was made by an Evangelism Explosion team, and the gospel was presented. Occasionally, for some, another type of approach was more effective.

Step Three. If interest was shown, the visitor was encouraged to return again—either with the friend who brought him the first time or with the one who contacted him. He was also invited to attend the church's Discovery Class, a five-week, intimate-sized course for the explanation of the basics of the Bible and the gospel, with opportunities given for the class members to receive Christ.

Step Four. The folding process continued after five weeks in the Discovery Class (which could be entered at any of the five sessions), as the newcomer was invited to attend an adult Sunday school class of his choice. These classes were also the bases for socializing, small-group activity, prayer "hot lines," and so on; they were places where the newcomer could be pulled into a sense of belonging, into relationships, and hopefully into a small group and into regular worship service attendance. (Always the aim was to establish the newcomer in the three levels of communication—"celebration," "congregation," and "cell.")

Step Five. The possibility of church membership was presented along this path as the newcomer seemed ready to become a believer. In the six-week membership class the church board would be monitoring his personal progress, to lead him to the conversion experience or to be assured that this had already taken place.

I truly believe that, although church membership can be overstressed, it can also be understressed. Church membership and baptism are both important for commitment to the local body!

Step Six. The folding process was completed when the new believer was not only established in the church's regular public worship, and in a Sunday school class for fellowship and care and instruction, but also in a home-based weekly small group as well, where close friendships could be established, his or her intimate needs could be met, and he or she could be held accountable for growth and progress.

24.

We've dealt with the first of the five ways a local church should grow: numerically. And incidentally, we never need be ashamed of concern over numbers! God loves people, and numbers represent individual people, with their hurts and their needs. The Word of God is full of numbers—how many people were fed on a mountain side, how many were saved at Pentecost, how the church grew soon after that, and so on.

The second way a local church should grow is through world missions. The healthy church must have a far-reaching vision for the world and a plan to infiltrate and influence that world. The leaders of the church owe it to their people to keep the Great Commission before them in knowledge and in practice. A missions focus is not an option to choose but a command to be obeyed!

This takes constant vigilance and care. The pastor himself must lead the way by giving, by praying, by preaching—perhaps by going—and certainly by encouraging a great spirit of generosity in the church, urging it to part with its money and its people for the great needs of the world.

This is not to say that the home base is to be neglected.

In fact the opposite is true; the home church must be strengthened in every way, because *what it is at home it will reproduce overseas.*

What if the home church is selfish, considering soft cushions ahead of Bibles in India? If by accident that home church gets reproduced overseas, the reproduction will also be selfish and its own vision only local.

On the other hand, three-priorities churches will plant three-priorities work around the world. A young person from a home church where worship is exciting will seek to reproduce that spirit of worship in the new place. A missionary from a loving small group in the home church will establish networks of small groups wherever he goes. The added bonus is that he'll have the assurance of half a dozen or so at home who pray for him and support him unceasingly. And when he comes home on furlough his group will be waiting to receive him again!

If Priority Two is truly Priority Two, missionaries supported by a church can't be people who show up in the pulpit every few years to give a report and then are never seen in between except as pictures tacked on a map. These supported missionaries must, for at least some period of the time, live among the home church members and be a real flesh-and-blood part of them, their children mingling with the home-church children. In this way, missions will become real to the home congregation and praying, giving, and going will be accelerated. Also, in this way, the missionaries will be able to take off their masks, be accepted as real people, and have their own personal needs met.

Some of the world's great missionary churches never have a "missionary conference," but they insist that their supported missionaries come out of their own congregation and spend time among them when on furlough. Then missions becomes not an annual affair but a continual emphasis.

25.

The third way a local church should grow is by planting baby churches. If healthy Christians are to reproduce themselves, so must healthy congregations!

The Lake Avenue Church planted a couple of baby churches over the years in haphazard ways. But under the guidance of one of its laymen, Lee Benuska, it experienced particular success in its latest effort.

This time, with great care and strategy, a task force studied the surrounding areas for the most needy and most possible site. The target area was established and visited door to door, and a roster of interested people from that neighborhood compiled. Then the Lake Avenue membership was surveyed for volunteers to become part of the baby church.

Simultaneously, Bob Ver Burg, a young man who had been born and raised in the mother church and who had just finished his seminary education, was taken onto the church staff for a year with general duties in many areas of the church life; the idea was to groom him as the possible first pastor of the baby church.

Next, a new Sunday school class was begun at Lake Avenue,

comprised of both the interested people from the new site (they traveled quite a distance to come to Lake Avenue for that period of time) and the Lake Avenue members who were considering transferring their allegiance to the new church. The class was named "The Little Church on the Third Floor," and Bob Ver Burg was assigned as its pastor-teacher. Like a human baby, this group gestated for nine months: about a hundred people in the womb of the mother church, snuggling together and getting comfortable with Bob and his wife Patti and with each other.

After meeting those nine months and forming small groups among themselves, the new church was launched at a Lake Avenue evening service with great celebration and prayer— and then on the following Sunday morning met for the first time as a new church in the target community.

Today, after several years, that church is a happy body of two hundred congregants. They have just added their first assistant pastor and wife, who were also out of the mother church and who therefore smoothly assist in carrying out the three-priorities philosophy of ministry.

The fourth way a local church should grow is by encouraging the existing churches around it. It's so important for the pastor and staff and lay leaders to openly pray for and promote the success of other churches in the area! Let your church take the initiative in starting a support group or several support groups for the pastors and church leaders of the community, so that each can be committed to the growth and well-being of the others.

Pastors everywhere are hurting, and probably many of them haven't even thought of the possibility of meeting in a small group, with other Christian leaders, to get relief and support. It means so much to me today to meet regularly in a group with brother pastors, and I know it means the same to them.

Another way of encouraging churches around you is to invite staff or leaders from local churches to come and minister to your church people. Sometimes pray for these churches by name in your pulpit. Take a team from your church if you're asked to speak to one of theirs. Occasionally have pulpit exchanges or joint-church conferences or even picnics together in the park! In these ways you'll not only be speaking kindly of the larger body of Christ, but also backing your sincere words with actions.

Fifth, every church must have a social conscience. Around your church are the poor, the mentally ill, the sick and elderly in convalescent homes, those in jails and prisons and hospitals, and the many suffering from family problems. Let the church train teams to minister locally and to lead the congregation in ministering to the various social concerns of its area.

One of the churches I served sent its young people to a county "old folks' home," where they led Aunt Nancy, aged ninety-eight, to know Christ. What a thrill it was for those kids to watch Aunt Nancy's spiritual progress! Aunt Nancy was permanently in bed and penniless, but one of the young people brought her an African violet. Soon Aunt Nancy had divided the violet plant into two pots, and then four, and then she was selling her violets from her bedside and sending the money to missions! When Aunt Nancy died several years later she was partially supporting a nurse in India, and our church high-schoolers could never be the same again.

Let your church stretch and grow and give itself away in social concerns of every kind. Enlarge your hearts as you see new needs here and new needs there!

My brother-in-law, Charles Parker Wright, pastored a Presbyterian church in downtown Atlanta. It is known for its loving concern. That church helps the poor. It helps the non-English-speaking newcomers to the city. It helps the drug addicts, the alcoholics, the pregnant single girls. It cooperates with Chuck Colson in helping prisoners. But it also reaches into private clubs and places of economic and political and educational power, because its heart is concerned for the upper class as well. In fact, it has established one of our country's most exclusive private schools—out of its concern to minister to the wealthy.

Let your church reach and reach—in all directions!

Part B:

The third priority in the private life of a church leader

26.

Church leader, you can't just love crowds! You have to learn to love people.

Oh, how God loves people! And if he is indeed your first priority and your heart is synchronized with his, then you will love people too, and you will lead your people in loving people!

God has a haunting love in his heart for the world. He forgets no one. And he wants to stretch your own heart to share his love.

See the resurrected Christ's full-orbed vision when the disciples asked him in Acts 1:6, "Lord, are you at this time going to restore the kingdom to Israel?"

Their concern was just for their own little nation. Jesus' reply was that it was not for them to know, but then he pushed their minds to take in larger horizons:

> But you will receive power when the Holy Spirit comes on you; and you will be my witnesses in Jerusalem, and in all Judea and Samaria, and to the ends of the earth.

Our Lord is not only the global Christ; Colossians says he is the cosmic Christ—whatever that means! Christ asks you to expand your vision to the whole world, and then he gives you an inheritance far larger than that!

But *people* are on his heart. Remember when the disciples were with Jesus for a day off, and five thousand men (how many women and children we don't know) suddenly came storming upon them. The Scriptures say that Jesus saw them as sheep without a shepherd, and he had compassion on them. They were guideless. They were leaderless. They were confused. And he loved them and his heart was moved toward them.

Whatever your gifts, Christian leader, let your heart be moved toward weary, confused *people.* The early Christians were filled with compassion for them:

"While they were speaking to the people . . ." (Acts 4:1). "The apostles were teaching the people . . ." (Acts 4:2). "The apostles performed many miraculous signs and wonders among the people . . ." (Acts 5:12).

For this the apostles were arrested and jailed, but God sent an angel and by miracle released them. Why? So that they could go back and again "tell the people the full message of this new life" (Acts 5:20)!

God loves people! And he is concerned that you love them too, that your heart stays warm and tender toward them.

F. B. Meyer, the famous British preacher, once spent a night as a house guest in the home of A. B. Simpson, the founder of the Christian and Missionary Alliance. Early the next morning Mr. Meyer stole downstairs, thinking he was the first one up.

But no; there, through the partially open door to the study, he could see Mr. Simpson in prayer. He had a world globe in front of him, and he would put his finger on a spot, and pray. Then he would spin it, put his finger on another spot, and pray.

Then, as F. B. Meyer watched unnoticed, A. B. Simpson

leaned forward and took the whole globe in his arms, and hugged it, and cried.

Is there built into your heart and into your lifestyle, Christian leader, a genuine, heartfelt reach to the world?

Epilogue

27.

It was years after God had given me the vision of the three priorities, as "handles" by which to measure and live the Christian life, that I read an article by Stanford Professor Jeffrey Pfeffer. Almost every line leaped off the page at me! I had known that the three priorities are *right,* but now I saw why they are such a powerful tool for leading a church or other Christian organization.

In his article, "Symbolism in Corporations," Dr. Pfeffer describes how business management, for a period beginning in the early fifties, revered analysis as its most important skill, because analysis measured facts and statistics, produced charts and graphs, and drew rational conclusions. The analysts were the "fair-haired boys," and the more statistics one could hold in his head, the more he impressed and awed his colleagues. But after several decades people got tired of boggled brains:

> The problem is not merely that human information-processing capacity is bounded, so that we are limited in the number of alternatives we can simultaneously consider and the data we can recall.

The problem is that there is an emotional, affective, nonrational side that is overlooked in the process. . . .

Much of the activity occurring in organizations is motivated more by sentiment than by rational calculation. Rationality is likely to be retrospective, so that we make sense out of what has already occurred. Thus, a task of leadership in organizations and in nations is to make activity meaningful and sensible and, in so doing, produce positive sentiments, attitudes, and feelings among those in the organization. In this pursuit, symbolism and symbolic activity, including the use of language, ceremonies, and settings, is all-important . . .[32]

Church leader, how do you describe your church—both to its members and to new visitors? In a larger church, old-time members may never know how many babies are cared for in the nursery, the process by which third-graders get prizes for memorizing Scripture, how often the organ gets tuned, what day of the week the bulletin must go to the printer, why new members cannot be immediately received as missionary candidates, or how the pastoral team is chosen. What are the most important things about your church that they should know?

And what should be said to newcomers? What should they know first about your church, as its most important ingredients? How many members you have? How much money you give annually to missions? Where the ladies' society meets on Wednesday noons? What your Sunday school curriculum is, or why it's the best? Where your choir director got his training?

And pastor or Christian leader, how do you describe the Christian life in a digestible form? What do you teach your new baby Christians first? Would you include grace versus works, the doctrines of the Second Coming, a quick history of the Old Testament, gifts and functions in the body of Christ, the final authority of Scripture? And how do you describe the Christian life to your old timers, so that in both doctrine and lifestyle they are a consistent whole, though allowing freedom for diversity on lesser issues?

Pfeffer says, "Because managers traffic so much in images,

the appropriate role for the manager may be evangelist rather
than accountant."[33] I think this is so. The church and the
Christian life need less to be dissected and analyzed and more
to be lived and "sold." *For this the basics need to be packaged
and visualized.*

Pfeffer quotes Louis Pondy:

> Suppose we think of leadership as a language. To practice, say,
> democratic leadership is to understand the set of meanings
> (values ?) to be conveyed, to give them primitive expression, to
> translate them into stylistic representation, and ultimately to
> choose sounds and actions that manifest them.
> The effectiveness of a leader lies in his ability to make activity
> meaningful for those in his role set . . . to give others a sense
> of understanding what they are doing and especially to articulate
> it so they can communicate about the meaning of their behavior.[34]

Everywhere around the world where I see Christians and
Christian churches seeking to live by the three priorities—in
my observation, at least—they are not reactionary, they're not
fussing over minor issues, they have a philosophy of ministry
which gives them happy freedom within definite boundaries.
They are seeking, in specific, creative, individual ways, how
to love the Lord, how to love their fellow believers, and how
to love the lost.

Says Pfeffer,

> [Symbols] convey meaning and emotion, and these, in turn,
> affect the way people think about what they do.[35]

The world of advertising knows this well. Very little effort
is put into explaining to the public precisely how coffee beans
are picked or processed, but thousands of dollars may be spent
to convey, "Folgers: ah-h-h!"

Pfeffer continues,

> Why is [symbolism] effective? Why do we tend to be taken in
> by labels, by settings, and by ceremonies? . . . We often don't
> really know our preferences; we often feel uncertain because of

the novel or strange settings of organizations . . . and given one's limited time and interest, symbols may be sufficient for reassurance.[36]

Christian leaders who thump prophecy or the study of the original biblical languages or the gifts of the Spirit above everything else will always find a contingent of followers—because multitudes of Christians know that Christianity is right, but they have no idea how to sort through the awesome maze of Christian information to know what is of prime importance. They want someone to sift it all through for them and give them a summary—something visual, some "hooks" on which to hang all the rest.

Dr. Pfeffer's "bottom line" (there I go, using a visual symbol to express my concept to you!) is this: "Themes . . . reinforced in a number of symbolic ways, are what seem to distinguish effective from less effective organizations."[37]

In this book on the three priorities I have not attempted critically to deal with such important aspects of our faith as the deity of the Lord Jesus Christ and the efficacy of his shed blood on the cross for us; the "blessed hope" of his sure return; the authority of the Holy Scriptures; the precious role of the Holy Spirit in our lives. The three priorities are not everything. They will not transform liberal theology or raise a man from the dead!

But they are symbols by which a church can get hold of itself, find its philosophy of ministry, eliminate the inconsequential and concentrate on what is eternally important. These three priorities are a powerful teaching tool by which to orient any individual Christian, any Christian family, and any local church or Christian school or mission organization or denomination. They give us a way to define ourselves—and more: if taken seriously enough to be acted on in visible, measurable ways, they become the means to a life of joy and power.

The morning that I first preached the three priorities to our congregation I provided a "ceremony," and Dr. Pfeffer confirms that this was important. I asked the people who would commit themselves to these three priorities in three tangible ways to sign cards.[38] Six hundred signed, and that day became a milestone in the life of our church; we knew we had turned a corner and started on a new journey together.

Christian leader, if you indeed are seeking the Lord's guidance in espousing these priorities as your church's or group's own philosophy of ministry, I strongly suggest that you plan some kind of attention-getting and instructional "ceremony." Perhaps you'll have a several-day period of time in which you'll teach your people what these three priorities involve, and then have some kind of concluding experience when together you commit yourselves.

28.

Eventually, given enough time, any organization becomes a reflection of its leader or leaders.

As I look around me here in Southern California, I see cities which have obviously had sharp, progressive leadership, and I see others whose city fathers must have just gotten crushed in the rush.

God has always ordained human leadership. Ehud came into a time of confusion in Israel: " 'Follow me,' he ordered" (Judg. 3:28)—and the resulting victories led to eighty years of peace.

Gideon said, "Watch me. . . . Follow my lead. . . . Do exactly as I do" (Judg. 7:17)—and three hundred Hebrews defeated thousands of Midianites.

The apostle Paul wrote, "Join with others in following my example, brothers" (Phil. 3:17). "Become like me" (Gal. 4:12; see also I Thess. 1:6, 2:10–12, and 2 Thess. 3:7–9).

A congregation becomes like its pastor and leadership to a scary degree! Intense leaders will raise up intense followers. Jokers will create congregations that laugh a lot. If the leaders' wives are sharp dressers, soon the church will be full of women who are sharp dressers!

On the other hand, if, for instance, the church leadership doesn't care how the church buildings and grounds look, after a while neither will the people. Hymnbooks will be stacked in corners, every cupboard will become a "lost-and-found" . . .

You've seen church bulletin boards go unchanged for weeks. A church our family used to drive by put on its bulletin board one May for Mothers' Day, "Do as Mother used to do: go to church on Sunday." It looked good over the summer, and not too bad with autumn colors around it, but by the time snow began to fall on it our children were shouting before we ever turned the corner and saw the sign, "Do as Mother used to do—" and they'd howl with laughter.

So the final challenge of this book is this: the three priorities are not a quick gimmick that will shape up a church when the church leaders are not willing first to live them out for themselves. Anne and I found years ago that if we challenged groups to the three priorities without having completely "sold" their leaders, the people would be doomed to eventual frustration. On the other hand, I think of the Peru Branch of Wycliffe Bible Translators to whom we ministered in 1972. Because Jerry Elder, their Branch Director, shepherded the missionaries in these three priorities by his own heart and life, the resulting renewal lasted for years.

In my own life as a Christian leader, these three priorities constantly challenge and stimulate me. Anne and I feel our lives so blessed for having defined as our first life-priority to relate to the very Person of the Lord himself in every way we can think of, and to encourage others to do the same! And yet I fail every day, and I cry, "O for a closer walk with God!"

Because I am naturally relational, I love encouraging and interacting with my brothers and sisters in Christ, so the second priority is easiest for me. In fact my strength sometimes becomes my weakness, and I get worn out from saying yes to too many people, when my soul needs to be alone again being restored in God.

The third priority is my weakest—at least in my personal evangelism. So because of my own consciousness of the three priorities and my desire to please him with a balanced life, the Holy Spirit prods me to witness, to go after the souls of men. And he helps me win souls when otherwise I might not.

The three priorities, then, prod me, challenge me, satisfy me, and balance me!

They specifically balance any day of my life. When I pause in the middle of a day to think, "What shall I do next?" I may ask, "Have I gotten time alone with God today?" No? Then that's next. "Have I in some way encouraged the body of Christ?" An activity in that direction should be next. "Has this day so far included any help for the lost?" . . .

And they balance my weeks, which are a more true measure of my total lifestyle. Some small groups I know critique themselves by writing out their week's schedule in detail and coloring all Priority One activities blue, all Priority Two activities red, all Priority Three activities green. Quickly they see what's neglected in their lives. This little project might also be an effective way to test the balance of a church's week, or a church's internal organization.

These priorities balance the thrust of any Christian body. Any group of believers must be constantly called back again to the Lord Jesus Christ himself, to love for him, attention to him, worship of him. He must not be assumed; he must be consciously *gathered around,* both publicly and privately. He is to be obeyed; because he is in fact the Head, he must set agenda for the local body. And he is to be enjoyed as the constant Companion of every believer.

As the body's Head, his first and overriding command to us is that we love one another, be committed to one another. Even the established habit of worshiping, admiring, and affirming him will release grace so that believers can learn to admire, lift, and affirm each other! And as they strengthen this second priority in their lives, Christ binds them together with himself in an eternal relationship.

Then, as the bond of love with Christ and each other is secured, comes success in folding in hurting, needy worldlings. The clear command of our Lord is to go to the world—but not in the context of coldness or dissension within the ranks of those who go. Out of the first priority must flow the second, and out of the second must flow the third.

The order of the priorities is important. Where a church or group is not first vertical, first rich in God, it will be thin and poor in its horizontal relationships. And when it is not a deeply, spiritually united team, exploits for God in the world will come very hard. I have seen wonderful spiritual renewal come to lonely, burned-out missionaries who gave themselves afresh to God and to each other.

Yet these priorities must be active all at once, and all the time. Let the Christian leader lead his people strongly in these three areas, and many unnecessary schemes and programs— weak, "quick answers" to things—will fall by the wayside. God's people will be caught up in what is eternally important.

Let's say it once more, strongly:

It is not enough to love the Lord. (I am not speaking of the minimum for salvation.)

It is not enough even to love the Lord and each other.

It is only enough to love the Lord, and to love his people, and to love his world, too.

I watched on television the 1980 Winter Olympics, and I saw that young American hockey team play the veteran Russians, shocking the world that day with a 4-3 victory.

As the game was nearing its end and the American team had taken the lead, the crowd was roaring with excitement. During the last moments the Russians, seeking a goal, were frantically skating around crashing into American players and trying to confuse them.

At that point the television focused on the American coach, pacing back and forth and shouting both to his men on the bench and his men on the ice. Over and over he cried, "Play your game! Play your game!" By this he meant that they must not let the Russians get them playing the game according to the Russians—and become confused. "Play your game! Play your game!" In that moment of high tension they must stick to the style they'd been taught, to the basic style with which they were familiar.

So it is with the church. It is absolutely essential that the leadership have a defined philosophy of ministry, that the people be thoroughly trained in it, and that together they stick to it. Then, through thick and thin, through hard times and good, the instinct will be there to major on the time-honored, Spirit-ordained, biblical basics.

Church of Jesus Christ, play your game! Play your game! Play your game!

If I can help you further, write to:

Ray Ortlund
Renewal Ministries
32 Whitewater Drive
Corona del Mar, CA   92625

NOTES

1. Peter Drucker on church management: "The Art of Doing the Important," *Church Management,* 1972, 5.
2. Marcus Dods, *The Expositor's Bible: The Book of Genesis* (London: Hodder and Stoughton, 1907), 131.
3. Ibid., 121.
4. Ezra Earl Jones, *Strategies for New Churches* (New York: Harper & Row, 1978), 17.
5. Raymond C. Ortlund, *Lord, Make My Life a Miracle* (Glendale, CA: Regal Books, 1974), 2–3.
6. Anne Ortlund, *Discipling One Another,* formerly titled *Love Me with Tough Love* (Waco, TX: Word Books, 1979), 69.
7. Anne Ortlund, *Up With Worship* (Glendale, CA: Regal Books, 1975), 27.
8. "Can Catholics Learn Anything from Evangelical Protestants?", *Christianity Today,* 18 December 1970, 12–14.
9. Raymond C. Ortlund, *Lord, Make My Life a Miracle,* 20–23.
10. Anne Ortlund, *Up With Worship,* 74–75.
11. *Christianity Today,* 19 December 1975, 22.
12. Alexander Whyte, *Lancelot Andrewes and His Private Devotions* (London: Oliphant, Anderson, and Ferrier, 1896), 103.
13. DeVern F. Fromke, *Ultimate Intention* (Mt. Vernon, MO: Sure Foundation Pub., 1962), 10.
14. Raymond C. Ortlund, *Lord, Make My Life a Miracle,* 13–15.
15. Vernard Eller, *The Simple Life* (Grand Rapids, MI: Wm. B. Eerdmans Publishing Co., 1973), 24, 27, 28.
16. *The Interpreter's Bible* (New York: Abingdon Press, 1951), 3:323.
17. D. Martin Lloyd-Jones, *Studies on the Sermon on the Mount,* vol. 2 (Grand Rapids, MI: Wm. B. Eerdmans Publishing Co., 1960), 143.
18. Jonathan Edwards, ed., *The Life and Diary of David Brainerd, 1744,* newly ed. by Philip E. Howard, Jr., (Chicago: Moody Press, Wycliffe Series of Christian Classics, 1949), 169.

19. Frederic W. H. Myers, *Saint Paul* (London: MacMillan and Co., 1907), 1.

20. Robert Robinson (1735–1790), "Come, Thou Fount of Ev'ry Blessing."

21. Thomas Kelly, *The Eternal Promise* (New York: Harper & Row, 1966), 22.

22. "Excerpts from Jim Elliot's Diary," *HIS,* April 1956, 9.

23. Charles Hummel, *The Tyranny of the Urgent* (Downers Grove, IL: InterVarsity Press, 1976), 5.

24. Anne Ortlund, *Up With Worship,* 26–30.

25. Francis Schaeffer, *The Church at the End of the Twentieth Century* (Downer's Grove, IL: InterVarsity Press, 1970), 136, 137.

26. Raymond C. Ortlund, *Lord, Make My Life a Miracle,* 59–70. See also Raymond C. Ortlund, *Intersections: With Christ at the Crossroads of Life* (Waco, TX: Word Books, 1979), 69–87.

27. Anne Ortlund, *Discipling One Another,* 111.

28. John Simon, *John Wesley and the Religions Societies* (London: Epworth Press, 1921), 196–198.

29. For more on these principles see Robert Coleman, *The Master Plan of Evangelism* (Englewood Cliffs, NJ: Fleming H. Revell Co., 1963).

30. Formerly titled *Love Me with Tough Love* (Waco, TX: Word Books, 1979).

31. Elton Trueblood, *The Lord's Prayer* (New York: Harper & Row, 1965), 36.

32. Jeffrey Pfeffer, "Symbolism in Corporations," *Stanford GBS Magazine* 50(Winter 1981):2,3.

33. Ibid., 3.

34. Ibid., 3.

35. Ibid., 5.

36. Ibid., 7.

37. Ibid., 7.

38. Raymond C. Ortlund, *Lord, Make My Life a Miracle,* 3.

STUDY GUIDE

1.1. Ortlund lists eight types of churches on pp. 9–10. Which "labels" best describe your church?

1.2. What is to be the church's chief function?

1.3. Read and discuss the scriptures cited on pp. 10–11.

1.4. What are the three priorities for the church (see p. 11)?

2.1. What's your reaction to the following: "It seems that churches are not so much in a crisis of organization as they are in a crisis of objectives" (p. 13)?

2.2. Do you agree that most *churches* "don't do the right things" (p. 13)?

2.3. Do you agree that most *pastors* "don't do the essential things" (p. 13)?

2.4. Do you believe that the church is equipped with every power to fulfill every obligation God has for it (p. 14)?

2.5. Reread and discuss the Spurgeon story at the end of this chapter.

3.1. Discuss the concept of "repeated" pastorates (p. 16).

3.2. What three commitments are to be priorities for the church (p. 17)?

3.3. How does Ortlund suggest we carry out these commitments?

3.4. Why is it important to keep the priorities in order, 1–2–3?

4.1. To whom should these priorities apply?

4.2. In what ways can you follow these three priorities?

4.3. Read John 15 for discussion.

4.4. How can everyone commit themselves to the three priorities?

5.1. Could your church successfully conduct its various committee meetings if the first half of the allotted meeting time were given to exercising the first two priorities?

5.2. How would you react to the so-called irritants?

5.3. What do you think of the idea that the three priorities are the lubricants of the ministry?

6.1. What distractions do you, your group, your church encounter in your efforts to focus on the three priorities?

6.2. In addition to the passages noted on pp. 26–28, do other scriptures come to your mind that underline the reality of the three priorities?

7.1. In what ways can you put Christ first in your corporate life?

7.2. What would happen to your church if all activity was halted for one week in order to "wait on God"?

7.3. Are you centering your life on Christ? Is your church?

8.1. Is your church "preoccupied" with its own existence?

8.2. Does your church advertise itself as if it were "selling" itself?

8.3. How do you describe your church to others?

9.1. Does worship occur at your church during the worship service?

9.2. What is the sequence of worship outlined in Isaiah 6?

9.3. How do you respond to the Whitman quotation on p. 39?

10.1. Are there any activities at your church that are contrary to your philosophy of ministry?

10.2. Is Christ in all your experience as he is in all your theology?

10.3. Can you pray the prayer similar to that of Lancelot Andrewes on p. 41?

11.1. If you have a leadership role in your church, do you feel that your leadership is Christ-centered, whole, and balanced?

11.2. If you do not have a leadership role in your church, do you feel that your discipleship is Christ-centered, whole, and balanced?

12.1. Are there reminders you can establish for yourself in order to check in with God?

12.2. If you are a pastor, how do you respond to the statement that "moment-by-moment seeking after God will lead people past [the preacher] to that same God"?

12.3. Do you feel comfortable meeting the Lord in his house in the company of his people?

12.4. Do you have a regular schedule of prayer?

12.5. Have you or other members of your church's leadership taken time for withdrawal for prayer and planning?

12.6. How clear is your focus during these times of withdrawal and renewal?

13.1. What are the four reasons given in Ephesians for the priority of the church?

13.2. When was the last time you sensed God's presence?
13.3. How important is your church to that sense of God's presence?
14.1. How important is church membership?
14.2. What kind of unity do you experience in your church?
15.1. How is love expressed in your church?
15.2. Do you express love and gratitude to those around you?
15.3. Has love or gratitude been expressed to you at church?
15.4. Is your church an organization or an organism?
15.5. Do you tend to think of other members according to their function only?
15.6. Do you tend to grade the "performance" of other church members?
15.7. Do you have a "function"?
16.1. What are the three levels of contact in the church?
16.2. How do you feel about generating a small group?
16.3 What does Ortlund recommend as the five-point agenda for these small groups?
17.1. Can you open up to other people without rules or guidelines?
18.1. Is your church unshockable, democratic, accepting?
18.2. Have you ever played Peter to someone's Paul?
18.3. Have you ever played Paul to someone's Peter?
19.1. Is the leadership of the church a discipling group?
19.2. Are families in the church discipling groups?
19.3. Are you and your family a discipling group?
19.4. What are the guidelines for discipling groups?
20.1. Are you as willing to be ministered to as you are to minister?
21.1. What are your thoughts about the three worshipers?
22.1. What are the three observations made about the story of the paralytic and his friends (Mark 2:1–12)?
22.2. What are the three priorities for small groups?
23.1. What are the five ways that a church should grow?
23.2. What are the six steps of nurturing new members of the church?
24.1. Does your church have a world view?
25.1. Does your church have plans to start other churches?
25.2. Does your church encourage other churches in the area?
25.3. Does your church have a social conscience?
26.1. How sensitive are you to the masses in need?

27.1. What are the most important things about your church that members and visitors should know?

27.2. How does your church express the knowledge of what it considers to be of prime importance?

28.1. How can you best "play your game" with the help of the three priorities?